FREE Test Taking Tips Video/DVD Offer

To better serve you, we created videos covering test taking tips that we want to give you for FREE. **These videos cover world-class tips that will help you succeed on your test.**

We just ask that you send us feedback about this product. Please let us know what you thought about it—whether good, bad, or indifferent.

To get your **FREE videos**, you can use the QR code below or email freevideos@studyguideteam.com with "Free Videos" in the subject line and the following information in the body of the email:

    a. The title of your product

    b. Your product rating on a scale of 1-5, with 5 being the highest

    c. Your feedback about the product

If you have any questions or concerns, please don't hesitate to contact us at info@studyguideteam.com.

Thank you!

SHSAT Prep Book 2023-2024

4 SHSAT Practice Tests with Math and ELA Study Guide for the New York City Exam [7th Edition]

Joshua Rueda

Interested in buying more than 10 copies of our product? Contact us about bulk discounts:
bulkorders@studyguideteam.com

ISBN 13: 9781637758472
ISBN 10: 1637758472

Table of Contents

Welcome

Dear Reader,

Welcome to your new Test Prep Books study guide! We are pleased that you chose us to help you prepare for your exam. There are many study options to choose from, and we appreciate you choosing us. Studying can be a daunting task, but we have designed a smart, effective study guide to help prepare you for what lies ahead.

Whether you're a parent helping your child learn and grow, a high school student working hard to get into your dream college, or a nursing student studying for a complex exam, we want to help give you the tools you need to succeed. We hope this study guide gives you the skills and the confidence to thrive, and we can't thank you enough for allowing us to be part of your journey.

In an effort to continue to improve our products, we welcome feedback from our customers. We look forward to hearing from you. Suggestions, success stories, and criticisms can all be communicated by emailing us at info@studyguideteam.com.

Sincerely,
Test Prep Books Team

FREE Videos/DVD OFFER

Doing well on your exam requires both knowing the test content and understanding how to use that knowledge to do well on the test. We offer completely FREE test taking tip videos. **These videos cover world-class tips that you can use to succeed on your test.**

To get your **FREE videos**, you can use the QR code below or email freevideos@studyguideteam.com with "Free Videos" in the subject line and the following information in the body of the email:

    a. The title of your product
    b. Your product rating on a scale of 1-5, with 5 being the highest
    c. Your feedback about the product

If you have any questions or concerns, please don't hesitate to contact us at info@studyguideteam.com.

SCAN HERE

Quick Overview

As your child or student draws closer to taking their exam, being prepared becomes more and more important. Thankfully, they have this study guide to help them get ready. Use this guide to help keep their studying on track and refer to it often.

This study guide contains several key sections that will help your child be successful on their exam. The guide has tips for what they should do the night before and the day of the test. Also included are test-taking tips. These tips will help equip them to read, assess, and answer test questions.

A large part of the guide is devoted to showing your child what content to expect on the exam and to helping them better understand that content. We also show them practice test questions so that they can see how well they understand the concept of the exam. Then, answer explanations are provided so that they can understand why they missed certain questions.

Your child shouldn't try to cram the night before their exam. First, their retention of the information will be low. Their time would be better used by reviewing information they already know rather than trying to learn a lot of new information. Second, they will likely become stressed as they try to gain a large amount of knowledge in a short amount of time. Third, they will be deprived of sleep. So be sure that your child goes to bed at a reasonable time the night before. Being well-rested helps them focus and remain calm.

Be sure that your child eats a substantial breakfast the morning of the exam. If they are taking the exam in the afternoon, be sure that they have a good lunch as well. Being hungry is distracting and can make it difficult to focus. They have hopefully spent lots of time preparing for the exam. Don't let an empty stomach get in the way of success!

Encourage your child to pace themself during the exam. They shouldn't rush. Your child should use all of the allotted time if needed.

Tell your child that it's important to remain positive while taking the exam even if they feel like they are performing poorly. Thinking about the content they should have mastered will not help them perform better on the exam.

Once the exam is complete, allow your child to take some time to relax. Even if they feel that they need to study for other things, they will be well served by some down time before they begin studying again. It's often easier to convince a child to study if they know that it will come with a reward!

Test-Taking Strategies

1. Predicting the Answer

When your child feels confident in their preparation for a multiple-choice test, they should try predicting the answer before looking at the answer choices. By predicting the answer before viewing the choices, they will less likely be distracted by an incorrect answer choice. They will feel more confident in their selection if they evaluate the question, predict the answer, and then find their prediction among the answer choices. After using this strategy, they should be sure to go through all of the answer choices carefully and completely. If your child feels unprepared, they should not attempt to predict the answers. This would be a waste of time and an opportunity for their mind to wander in the wrong direction.

2. Examine the Whole Question

Too often, test takers scan a multiple-choice question and immediately jump to the answer choices. Test authors are aware of this common impatience, and they will sometimes prey upon it. A test author will include answer choices that would seem correct if the question isn't fully understood. The only way to avoid falling into this trap is to examine the whole question carefully before looking at the answer choices. The CogAT and NNAT exams specifically focus on the ability of the test taker to analyze the relationship between all of the components of a question in order to find the correct answer. Therefore, it is crucial that you encourage your child to study an entire question before moving on to the answer choices.

3. Looking for Wrong Answers

One way to simplify a multiple-choice question is to eliminate all of the answer choices that are clearly wrong. There will usually be at least one choice that can be dismissed right away. Once the obviously incorrect answers have been eliminated, the remaining choices may be considered.

4. Don't Overanalyze

When individuals are nervous, their brains will often run wild, causing them to make associations and discover clues that don't exist. If you feel that this may be a problem for your child, remind them that they should do whatever they can to slow down during the test. They can try taking a deep breath or counting to ten. They should also be sure to not overthink the question. The associations that are shown in the question should lead your child to figure out the answer, so they need to be sure that the associations or clues that they are using when looking for an answer are derived from the question and not from their imagination.

5. No Need for Panic

It is wise to learn as many strategies as possible before taking a multiple-choice test, but it is likely that your child will come across a few questions for which they don't know the answer. In this situation, they should avoid panicking. Getting one incorrect answer does not mean failure. When they find a question that they either don't understand or don't know how to answer, they should take a deep breath and just do their best. Encourage your child to look over the entire question slowly and carefully. Then, they should read all of the answer choices carefully. After eliminating obviously wrong answers, they can

3

make a selection and move on to the next question.

6. First Instinct

Many people struggle with multiple-choice tests because they overthink the questions. If your child has studied for their test and understands the format of the test, they should be prepared to trust their first instinct once they have evaluated the question and the answer choices. There is a great deal of research suggesting that the mind can come to the correct conclusion quickly once it has obtained all of the relevant information. At times, it may seem as if one's intuition is working faster than one's reasoning mind. This may in fact be true. The student should verify their instinct by working out the reasons that it should be trusted.

7. Reading Every Answer Choice

It may seem obvious, but your child should always look at every one of the answer choices! Too many test takers fall into the habit of scanning the question and assuming that they understand the question. From there, they pick the first answer choice that seems correct. Test takers who look over and analyze all of the answer choices might discover that one of the latter answer choices is actually *more* correct. Moreover, looking at all of the answer choices might remind the student of an observation they made when looking at the question. This could help them arrive at the correct answer. Sometimes, an incorrect detail in one of the latter answer choices will trigger their memory and enable them to find the right answer. Failing to consider all of the answer choices is like not reading all of the items on a restaurant menu: your child might miss out on the perfect choice.

8. Rephrasing to Understand

Sometimes, a question on a multiple-choice test is difficult not because of what it asks but because of how it is written. If this is the case, the question or answer choices can be viewed in different ways, such as looking at the question from right to left rather than only from left to right. This process serves a couple of important purposes. First, it forces the student to concentrate on the core of the question so that they can understand it well. Mentally "rephrasing" the question by viewing and analyzing the patterns in a different order will concentrate their mind on the key patterns and relationships in the question. Second, it will present the information to their mind in a fresh way. This process may trigger them to discover a connection that they didn't observe before.

9. No Patterns

Answer choices will never be chosen based on patterns. The questions are scrambled and delivered in a random order. Any attempt to discern a pattern in the answer choices is a waste of time and a distraction from the real work of taking the test.

Bonus Content

We host multiple bonus items online, including all four practice tests in digital format. Scan the QR code or go to this link to access this content:

testprepbooks.com/bonus/shsat

The first time you access the page, you will need to register as a "new user" and verify your email address.

If you have any issues, please email support@testprepbooks.com.

Introduction to the SHSAT

Function of the Test

The SHSAT is a standardized test that is used as the sole factor for admission to eight of New York City's Specialized High Schools. Fiorello H. LaGuardia High School is the only Specialized High School in New York City that does not require students to take the SHSAT exam as part of the admissions process. Students who are in the eighth or ninth grades who wish to attend one of these eight Specialized High Schools and who live in the five boroughs of New York City (Brooklyn, Manhattan, Queens, Staten Island, and The Bronx) must sit for this exam.

Test Administration

Each year, the SHSAT test is only offered in the month of October for eighth grade students and in the month of November for ninth grade students. Students who are interested in registering to take the exam can do so by talking with their school's guidance counselor. After students are registered, they will receive a test ticket to sit for the exam. Students who are sitting for the SHSAT exam must also rank (in order of priority) the Specialized High Schools that they would like to attend on their test ticket.

Students are able to take the SHSAT test twice—once in the eighth grade and once in the ninth grade—if they are not accepted to the Specialized High School of their choice after taking the exam in the eighth grade.

Students will be provided with the necessary accommodations for taking the exam, as long as the accommodations are permitted for the test. If necessary, mathematics glossaries can be provided in nine languages to students on the day of the exam.

Test Format

Students are given 180 minutes to complete the SHSAT, which is comprised of 57 questions in each of its two sections: English language arts (ELA) and math, as outlined in the table. All of the reading and writing questions in the ELA section are multiple-choice and split between two categories. The first category requires students to utilize their revising and editing skills, while the second category assesses reading comprehension by asking students to extract information from various reading passages in order to answer associated questions. In the math section, there are 52 multiple-choice questions that deal with word and computational problems, as well as five grid-in questions that are *not* multiple-choice. These questions require students to provide correct numerical solutions to computational problems. Finally, all multiple-choice questions on both sections of the test have four answer choices per question, and both sections of the test each have ten unscored experimental questions that are used for field testing purposes for future iterations of the exam.

Sections of the SHSAT Test				
Subject Areas	**Questions (Multiple-Choice)***	**Question breakdown**		**Time Limit**
English Language Arts (ELA) Reading & Writing	57	9-11 revising/editing		180 minutes
		46-48 reading comprehension questions 3-4 informational passages 1-2 literary prose passages 1 poem		
		10 embedded field questions (unscored)		
Math	57	52 word & computational problems		
		5 grid-in questions*		
		10 embedded field questions (unscored)		
Total Questions:	114			

Students are required to provide correct numerical answers for these questions

Scoring

Individuals are not penalized for wrong answers or for questions that are left blank. After completing the test, each student is given a raw score that is based on the number of questions answered correctly. Those raw scores are then converted into three-digit composite scores (an 800 being the highest possible score). Scores are made available to the schools in March following the fall in which the exam was taken. For example, if a student takes the exam in the fall of 2020, their score will be released to the schools in the March of 2021.

Once the test results are in, all students who took the SHSAT exam are ranked in order by composite score from highest to lowest. Seats are then filled in each of the Specialized High Schools, in order, according to the students' first choices until all of the open seats for that academic year are filled. The number of available seats at each of the Specialized High Schools varies from year to year.

Recent/Future Developments

The SHSAT was revised in 2018 with changes mainly to the English language arts (ELA) section. The amount of questions in the Revising/Editing section decreased from 20 to 9-11. The Reading Comprehension section previously included primarily informational texts to analyze. The update now includes informational passages as well as literary prose passages and one poem on which questions are based.

Study Prep Plan for the SHSAT

1 **Schedule -** Use one of our study schedules below or come up with one of your own.

2 **Relax -** Test anxiety can hurt even the best students. There are many ways to reduce stress. Find the one that works best for you.

3 **Execute -** Once you have a good plan in place, be sure to stick to it.

One Week Study Schedule

Day 1	English Language Arts
Day 2	Revising/Editing
Day 3	Math
Day 4	Probability and Statistics
Day 5	SHSAT Practice Tests #1 & #2
Day 6	SHSAT Practice Tests #3 & #4
Day 7	Take Your Exam!

Two Week Study Schedule

Day 1	English Language Arts	Day 8	Answer Explanations for Practice Test #1
Day 2	Revising/Editing	Day 9	SHSAT Practice Test #2
Day 3	Math	Day 10	Answer Explanations for Practice Test #2
Day 4	Writing Expressions in Equivalent Forms	Day 11	SHSAT Practice Test #3
Day 5	Probability and Statistics	Day 12	Answer Explanations for Practice Test #3
Day 6	Geometry and Measurements	Day 13	SHSAT Practice Test #4
Day 7	SHSAT Practice Test #1	Day 14	Take Your Exam!

One Month Study Schedule

Day 1	English Language Arts	Day 11	Choosing a Level of Accuracy	Day 21	Surface Area and Volume Formulas
Day 2	Identifying Literary Elements	Day 12	Algebra	Day 22	SHSAT Practice Test #1
Day 3	Understanding Poetic Devices and Structure	Day 13	Finding the Zeros of a Function	Day 23	Answer Explanations for Practice Test #1
Day 4	Understanding the CharacteristicS...	Day 14	Methods for Solving Equations	Day 24	SHSAT Practice Test #2
Day 5	Revising/Editing	Day 15	Representing and Solving Equations...	Day 25	Answer Explanations for Practice Test #2
Day 6	Punctuation	Day 16	Function and Function Notation	Day 26	SHSAT Practice Test #3
Day 7	Word Usage	Day 17	Probability and Statistics	Day 27	Answer Explanations for Practice Test #3
Day 8	Sentence Fluency	Day 18	Representing Data	Day 28	SHSAT Practice Test #4
Day 9	Math	Day 19	Geometry and Measurements	Day 29	Answer Explanations for Practice Test #4
Day 10	Rewriting Expressions Involving Radicals...	Day 20	Properties of Polygons and Circles	Day 30	Take Your Exam!

Build your own prep plan by visiting:

testprepbooks.com/prep

As you study for your test, we'd like to take the opportunity to remind you that you are capable of great things! With the right tools and dedication, you truly can do anything you set your mind to. The fact that you are holding this book right now shows how committed you are. In case no one has told you lately, you've got this! Our intention behind including this coloring page is to give you the chance to take some time to engage your creative side when you need a little brain-break from studying. As a company, we want to encourage people like you to achieve their dreams by providing good quality study materials for the tests and certifications that improve careers and change lives. As individuals, many of us have taken such tests in our careers, and we know how challenging this process can be. While we can't come alongside you and cheer you on personally, we can offer you the space to recall your purpose, reconnect with your passion, and refresh your brain through an artistic practice. We wish you every success, and happy studying!

English Language Arts

Reading Comprehension

Main Ideas and Supporting Details

Topics and main ideas are critical parts of writing. The **topic** is the subject matter of the piece. An example of a topic would be global warming.

The **main idea** is what the writer wants to say about that topic. A writer may make the point that global warming is a growing problem that must be addressed in order to save the planet. Therefore, the topic is global warming, and the main idea is that it's a serious problem needing to be addressed. The topic can be expressed in a word or two, but the main idea should be a complete thought.

An author will likely identify the topic immediately within the title or the first sentence of a passage. The main idea is usually presented in the introduction. In a single passage, the main idea may be identified in the first or last sentence, but it will most likely be directly stated and easily recognized by the reader. Because it is not always stated immediately in a passage, it's important to carefully read the entire passage to identify the main idea.

The main idea should not be confused with the thesis statement. A **thesis statement** is a clear statement of the writer's specific stance and can often be found in the introduction of a non-fiction piece. The thesis is a specific sentence (or two) that offers the direction and focus of the discussion.

In order to illustrate the main idea, a writer will use **supporting details**, the details that provide evidence or examples to help make a point. Supporting details often appear in the form of quotations, paraphrasing, or analysis. Authors should connect details and analysis to the main point.

For example, in the example of global warming, where the author's main idea is to show the seriousness of this growing problem and the need for change, the use of supporting details in this piece would be critical in effectively making that point. Supporting details used here might include statistics on an increase in global temperatures and studies showing the impact of global warming on the planet. The author could also include projections for future climate change in order to illustrate potential lasting effects of global warming.

It's important to evaluate the author's supporting details to be sure that they are credible, provide evidence of the author's point, and directly support the main idea. Though shocking statistics grab readers' attention, their use could be ineffective information in the piece. Details like this are crucial to understanding the passage and evaluating how well the author presents their argument and evidence.

Also remember that when most authors write, they want to make a point or send a message. This point or message of a text is known as the theme. Authors may state themes explicitly, like in *Aesop's Fables*. More often, especially in modern literature, readers must infer the theme based on text details. Usually after carefully reading and analyzing an entire text, the reader can identify the theme. Typically, the longer the piece, the more themes you will encounter, though often one theme dominates the rest, as evidenced by the author's purposeful revisiting of it throughout the passage.

11

Summarizing a Complex Text

A **summary** is a shortened version of the original text, written by the reader in their own words. In order to effectively summarize a more complex text, it is necessary to fully understand the original source, and to highlight the major points covered. It may be helpful to outline the original text to get a big picture view of it, and to avoid getting bogged down in the minor details. For example, a summary wouldn't need to include a specific statistic from the original source unless it was the major focus of the piece. Also, it's important for readers to use their own words but to retain the original meaning of the passage. The key to a good summary is to emphasize the main idea without changing the focus of the original information.

Paraphrasing calls for the reader to take a small part of the passage and list or describe its main points. Paraphrasing is more than rewording the original passage, though. As with summary, a paraphrase should be written in the reader's own words, while still retaining the meaning of the original source. The main difference between summarizing and paraphrasing is the length of the original passage. A summary would be appropriate for a much larger piece, while paraphrase might focus on just a few lines of text. Effective paraphrasing will indicate an understanding of the original source, yet still help the reader expand on their interpretation. A paraphrase should neither add new information nor remove essential facts that will change the meaning of the source.

Recognizing the Structure of Texts

Writing can be classified under four passage types: narrative, expository, descriptive (sometimes called technical), and persuasive. Though these types are not mutually exclusive, one form tends to dominate the rest. By recognizing the *type* of passage you're reading, you gain insight into *how* you should read. If you're reading a narrative, you can assume the author intends to entertain, which means you may skim the text without losing meaning. A technical document might require a close read because skimming the passage might cause the reader to miss salient details.

1. **Narrative writing**, at its core, is the art of storytelling. For a narrative to exist, certain elements must be present. First, it must have characters. While many characters are human, characters could be defined as anything that thinks, acts, and talks like a human. For example, many recent movies, such as *Lord of the Rings* and *The Chronicles of Narnia*, include animals, fantastical creatures, and even trees that behave like humans. Second, it must have a plot or sequence of events. Typically, those events follow a standard plot diagram, but recent trends start *in medias res* or in the middle (near the climax). In this instance, foreshadowing and flashbacks often fill in plot details. Finally, along with characters and a plot, there must also be conflict. Conflict is usually divided into two types: internal and external. Internal conflict indicates the character is in turmoil and is presented through the character's thoughts. External conflicts are visible. Types of external conflict include a person versus nature, another person, or society.

2. **Expository writing** *is detached and to the point. Since expository* writing is designed to instruct or inform, it usually involves directions and steps written in second person ("you" voice) and lacks any persuasive or narrative elements. Sequence words such as *first*, *second*, and *third*, or *in the first place*, *secondly*, and *lastly* are often given to add fluency and cohesion. Common examples of expository writing include instructor's lessons, cookbook recipes, and repair manuals.

3. Due to its empirical nature, **technical writing** is filled with steps, charts, graphs, data, and statistics. The goal of technical writing is to advance understanding in a field through the scientific method.

12

Experts such as teachers, doctors, or mechanics use words unique to the profession in which they operate. These words, which often incorporate acronyms, are called *jargon*. Technical writing is a type of expository writing but is not meant to be understood by the general public. Instead, technical writers assume readers have received a formal education in a particular field of study and need no explanation as to what the jargon means. Imagine a doctor trying to understand a diagnostic reading for a car or a mechanic trying to interpret lab results. Only professionals with proper training will fully comprehend the text.

4. **Persuasive writing** is designed to change opinions and attitudes. The topic, stance, and arguments are found in the thesis, positioned near the end of the introduction. Later supporting paragraphs offer relevant quotations, paraphrases, and summaries from primary or secondary sources, which are then interpreted, analyzed, and evaluated. The goal of persuasive writers is not to stack quotes but to develop original ideas by using sources as a starting point. Good persuasive writing makes powerful arguments with valid sources and thoughtful analysis. Poor persuasive writing is riddled with bias and logical fallacies. Sometimes logical and illogical arguments are sandwiched together in the same piece. Therefore, readers should display skepticism when reading persuasive arguments.

Understanding Literary Interpretation

Literary interpretation is an interpretation and analysis of a literary work, based on the textual evidence in the work. It is often subjective as critical readers may discern different meanings in the details. A test taker needs to be prepared for questions that will test how well he or she can read a passage, make an analysis, and then provide evidence to support that analysis.

Literal and Figurative Meanings

When analyzing and interpreting fiction, readers must be active participants in the experience. Some authors make their messages clearer than others, but the onus is on the reader to add layers to what is read through interpretation. In literary interpretation, the goal is not to offer an opinion as to the inherent value of the work. Rather, the goal is to determine what the text means by analyzing the literal and figurative meanings of the text through critical reading.

Critical reading is close reading that elicits questions as the reader progresses. Many authors of fiction use literary elements and devices to further theme and to speak to their audience. These elements often utilize language that has an alternate or figurative meaning in addition to their actual or literal meaning. Readers should be asking questions about these and other important details as a passage is analyzed. What unfamiliar words are there? What is their contextual definition? How do they contribute to the overall feel of the work? How do they contribute to the mood and general message?

Drawing Inferences

An **inference** refers to a point that is implied (as opposed to directly-stated) by the evidence presented. It's necessary to use inference in order to draw conclusions about the meaning of a passage. Authors make implications through character dialogue, thoughts, effects on others, actions, and looks.

When making an inference about a passage, it's important to rely only on the information that is provided in the text itself. This helps readers ensure that their conclusions are valid.

Textual Evidence

It's helpful to read a passage a few times, noting details that seem important to the piece. Textual evidence helps readers draw a conclusion about a passage. **Textual evidence** refers to information—

13

facts and examples that support the main idea. Textual evidence will likely come from outside sources and can be in the form of quoted or paraphrased material. In order to draw a conclusion from evidence, it's important to examine the credibility and validity of that evidence as well as how (and if) it relates to the main idea. Effective use of textual evidence should connect to the main idea and support a specific point.

Understanding the Development of Themes

Identifying Theme or Central Message

The **theme** is the central message of a fictional work, whether that work is structured as prose, drama, or poetry. It is the heart of what an author is trying to say to readers through the writing, and theme is largely conveyed through literary elements and techniques.

In literature, a theme can often be determined by considering the overarching narrative conflict within the work. Though there are several types of conflicts and several potential themes within them, the following are the most common:

- *Individual against the self*—relevant to themes of self-awareness, internal struggles, pride, coming of age, facing reality, fate, free will, vanity, loss of innocence, loneliness, isolation, fulfillment, failure, and disillusionment

- *Individual against nature*— relevant to themes of knowledge vs. ignorance, nature as beauty, quest for discovery, self-preservation, chaos and order, circle of life, death, and destruction of beauty

- *Individual against society*— relevant to themes of power, beauty, good, evil, war, class struggle, totalitarianism, role of men/women, wealth, corruption, change vs. tradition, capitalism, destruction, heroism, injustice, and racism

- *Individual against another individual*— relevant to themes of hope, loss of love or hope, sacrifice, power, revenge, betrayal, and honor

For example, in Hawthorne's *The Scarlet Letter*, one possible narrative conflict could be the individual against the self, with a relevant theme of internal struggles. This theme is alluded to through characterization—Dimmesdale's moral struggle with his love for Hester and Hester's internal struggles with the truth and her daughter, Pearl. It's also alluded to through plot—Dimmesdale's suicide and Hester helping the very townspeople who initially condemned her.

Sometimes, a text can convey a message or universal lesson—a truth or insight that the reader infers from the text, based on analysis of the literary and/or poetic elements. This message is often presented as a statement. For example, a potential message in Shakespeare's *Hamlet* could be "Revenge is what ultimately drives the human soul." This message can be immediately determined through plot and characterization in numerous ways, but it can also be determined through the setting of Norway, which is bordering on war.

How Authors Develop Theme

Authors employ a variety of techniques to present a theme. They may compare or contrast characters, events, places, ideas, or historical or invented settings to speak thematically. They may use analogies, metaphors, similes, allusions, or other literary devices to convey the theme. An author's use of diction, syntax, and tone can also help convey the theme. Authors will often develop themes through the development of characters, use of the setting, repetition of ideas, use of symbols, and through contrasting value systems. Authors of both fiction and nonfiction genres will use a variety of these techniques to develop one or more themes.

Regardless of the literary genre, there are commonalities in how authors, playwrights, and poets develop themes or central ideas.

Authors often do research, the results of which contribute to theme. In prose fiction and drama, this research may include real historical information about the setting the author has chosen or include elements that make fictional characters, settings, and plots seem realistic to the reader. In nonfiction, research is critical since the information contained within this literature must be accurate.

In fiction, authors present a narrative conflict that will contribute to the overall theme. This conflict may involve the storyline itself and some trouble within characters that needs resolution. In nonfiction, this conflict may be an explanation or commentary on factual people and events.

Authors will sometimes use character motivation to convey theme, such as in the example from *Hamlet* regarding revenge. In fiction, the characters an author creates will think, speak, and act in ways that effectively convey the theme to readers. In nonfiction, the characters are factual, as in a biography, but authors pay particular attention to presenting those motivations to make them clear to readers.

Authors also use literary devices as a means of conveying theme. For example, the use of moon symbolism in Mary Shelley's *Frankenstein* is significant as its phases can be compared to the phases that the Creature undergoes as he struggles with his identity.

The selected point of view can also contribute to a work's theme. The use of first-person point of view in a fiction or non-fiction work engages the reader's response differently than third person point of view. The central idea or theme from a first-person narrative may differ from a third-person limited text.

In literary nonfiction, authors usually identify the purpose of their writing, which differs from fiction, where the general purpose is to entertain. The purpose of nonfiction is usually to inform, persuade, or entertain the audience. The stated purpose of a non-fiction text will drive how the central message or theme, if applicable, is presented.

Authors identify an audience for their writing, which is critical in shaping the theme of the work. For example, the audience for J.K. Rowling's *Harry Potter* series would be different than the audience for a biography of George Washington. The audience an author chooses to address is closely tied to the purpose of the work. The choice of an audience also drives the choice of language and level of diction an author uses. Ultimately, the intended audience determines the level to which that subject matter is presented and the complexity of the theme.

Identifying Literary Elements

There is no one, final definition of what literary elements are. They can be considered features or characteristics of fiction, but they are really more of a way that readers can examine a text for the purpose of analysis and understanding the meaning. The elements contribute to a reader's literary interpretation of a passage as to how they function to convey the central message of a work. The most common literary elements used for analysis are presented below.

15

Point of View

The **point of view** is the position the narrator takes when telling the story in prose. If a narrator is incorporated in a drama, the point of view may vary; in poetry, point of view refers to the position the speaker in a poem takes.

First Person

The first person point-of-view is when the writer uses the word "I" in the text. Poetry often uses first person, e.g., William Wordsworth's "I Wandered Lonely as a Cloud." Two examples of prose written in first person are Suzanne Collins's *The Hunger Games* and Anthony Burgess's *A Clockwork Orange*.

Second Person

The second person point of view is when the writer uses the pronoun *you*. It is not widely used in prose fiction, but as a technique, it has been used by writers such as William Faulkner in *Absalom, Absalom!* and Albert Camus in *The Fall*. It is more common in poetry—e.g., Pablo Neruda's "If You Forget Me."

Third Person

Third person point of view is when the writer utilizes pronouns such as him, her, or them. It may be the most utilized point of view in prose as it provides flexibility to an author and is the one with which readers are most familiar. There are two main types of third person used in fiction. **Third person omniscient** uses a narrator that is all-knowing, relating the story by conveying and interpreting thoughts/feelings of all characters. In **third person limited**, the narrator relates the story through the perspective of one character's thoughts/feelings, usually the main character.

Plot

The **plot** is what happens in the story. Plots may be singular, containing one problem, or they may be very complex, with many sub-plots. All plots have an exposition, a conflict, a climax, and a resolution. The **conflict** drives the plot and is something that the reader expects to be resolved. The plot carries those events along until there is a resolution to the conflict.

Tone

The **tone** of a story reflects the author's attitude and opinion about the subject matter of the story or text. Tone can be expressed through word choice, imagery, figurative language, syntax, and other details. The emotion or mood the reader experiences relates back to the tone of the story. Some examples of possible tones are humorous, somber, sentimental, and ironic.

Setting

The **setting** is the time, place, or set of surroundings in which the story occurs. It includes time or time span, place(s), climates, cultural environments, or geography—man-made or natural. Emily Dickinson's poem "Because I could not stop for Death" has a simple setting—the narrator's symbolic ride with Death through town towards the local graveyard. Conversely, Leo Tolstoy's *War and Peace* encompasses numerous settings within settings in the areas affected by the Napoleonic Wars, spanning from 1805 to 1812.

Characters

Characters are the story's figures that assume primary, secondary, or minor roles. Central or major characters are those who are integral to the story—the plot cannot be resolved without them. A central character can be a **protagonist** or hero. There may be more than one protagonist, and they don't always

16

have to possess good characteristics. A character can also be an **antagonist**—the force against a protagonist.

Character development is when the author takes the time to create dynamic characters that add uniqueness and depth to the story. *Dynamic* characters are characters that change over the course of the plot. Stock characters are those that appear across genres and embrace stereotypes—e.g., the cowboy of the Wild West or the blonde bombshell in a detective novel. A flat character is one that does not present a lot of complexity or depth, while a rounded character does. Sometimes, the narrator of a story or the speaker in a poem can be a character—e.g., Nick Carraway in F. Scott Fitzgerald's *The Great Gatsby* or the speaker in Robert Browning's "My Last Duchess." The narrator might also function as a character in prose, though not be part of the story—e.g., Charles Dickens's narrator of *A Christmas Carol*.

Figurative Language

Whereas literal language is the author's use of precise words, proper meanings, definitions, and phrases that mean exactly what they say, **figurative language** deviates from precise meaning and word definition—often in conjunction with other familiar words and phrases—to paint a picture for the reader. Figurative language is less explicit and more open to reader interpretation.

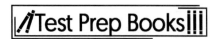

Some examples of figurative language are included in the following graphic.

	Definition	Example
Simile	Compares two things using "like" or "as"	Her hair was like gold.
Metaphor	Compares two things as if they are the same	He was a giant teddy bear.
Idiom	Using words with predictable meanings to create a phrase with a different meaning	The world is your oyster.
Alliteration	Repeating the same beginning sound or letter in a phrase for emphasis	The busy baby babbled.
Personification	Attributing human characteristics to an object or an animal	The house glowered menacingly with a dark smile.
Foreshadowing	Giving an indication that something is going to happen later in the story	I wasn't aware at the time, but I would come to regret those words.
Symbolism	Using symbols to represent ideas and provide a different meaning	The ring represented the bond between us.
Onomatopoeia	Using words that imitate sound	The tire went off with a bang and a crunch.
Imagery	Appealing to the senses by using descriptive language	The sky was painted with red and pink and streaked with orange.
Hyperbole	Using exaggeration not meant to be taken literally	The girl weighed less than a feather.

Figurative language can be used to give additional insight into the theme or message of a text by moving beyond the usual and literal meaning of words and phrases. It can also be used to appeal to the senses of readers and create a more in-depth story.

Understanding Poetic Devices and Structure

Poetic Devices

Rhyme is the poet's use of corresponding word sounds in order to create an effect. Most rhyme occurs at the ends of a poem's lines, which is how readers arrive at the rhyme scheme. Each line that has a corresponding rhyming sound is assigned a letter—A, B, C, and so on. When using a rhyme scheme, poets will often follow lettered patterns. Robert Frost's *"The Road Not Taken"* uses the ABAAB rhyme scheme:

Two roads diverged in a yellow wood,	A
And sorry I could not travel both	B
And be one traveler, long I stood	A
And looked down one as far as I could	A
To where it bent in the undergrowth;	B

18

Another important poetic device is **rhythm**—metered patterns within poetry verses. When a poet develops rhythm through meter, he or she is using a combination of stressed and unstressed syllables to create a sound effect for the reader.

Rhythm is created by the use of poetic feet—individual rhythmic units made up of the combination of stressed and unstressed syllables. A line of poetry is made up of one or more poetic feet. There are five standard types in English poetry, as depicted in the chart below.

Foot Type	Rhythm	Pattern
Iamb	buh Buh	Unstressed/stressed
Trochee	Buh buh	Stressed/unstressed
Spondee	Buh Buh	Stressed/stressed
Anapest	buh buh Buh	Unstressed/unstressed/stressed
Dactyl	Buh buh buh	Stressed/unstressed/unstressed

Structure

Poetry is most easily recognized by its structure, which varies greatly. For example, a structure may be strict in the number of lines it uses. It may use rhyming patterns or may not rhyme at all. There are three main types of poetic structures:

- *Verse*—poetry with a consistent meter and rhyme scheme
- *Blank verse*—poetry with consistent meter but an inconsistent rhyme scheme
- *Free verse*—poetry with inconsistent meter or rhyme

Verse poetry is most often developed in the form of stanzas—groups of word lines. Stanzas can also be considered verses. The structure is usually formulaic and adheres to the protocols for the form. For example, the English sonnet form uses a structure of fourteen lines and a variety of different rhyming patterns. The English ode typically uses three ten-line stanzas and has a particular rhyming pattern.

Poets choose poetic structure based on the effect they want to create. Some structures—such as the ballad and haiku—developed out of cultural influences and common artistic practice in history, but in more modern poetry, authors choose their structure to best fit their intended effect.

Understanding the Effect of Word Choice

An author's choice of words—also referred to as **diction**—helps to convey their meaning in a particular way. Through diction, an author can convey a particular tone—e.g., a humorous tone, a serious tone—in order to support the thesis in a meaningful way to the reader.

Connotation and Denotation

Connotation is when an author chooses words or phrases that invoke ideas or feelings other than their literal meaning. An example of the use of connotation is the word *cheap*, which suggests something is poor in value or negatively describes a person as reluctant to spend money. When something or someone is described this way, the reader is more inclined to have a particular image or feeling about it or him/her. Thus, connotation can be a very effective language tool in creating emotion and swaying opinion. However, connotations are sometimes hard to pin down because varying emotions can be associated with a word. Generally, though, connotative meanings tend to be fairly consistent within a specific cultural group.

Denotation refers to words or phrases that mean exactly what they say. It is helpful when a writer wants to present hard facts or vocabulary terms with which readers may be unfamiliar. Some examples of denotation are the words inexpensive and frugal. *Inexpensive* refers to the cost of something, not its value, and *frugal* indicates that a person is conscientiously watching their spending. These terms do not elicit the same emotions that *cheap* does.

Authors sometimes choose to use both, but what they choose and when they use it is what critical readers need to differentiate. One method isn't inherently better than the other; however, one may create a better effect, depending upon an author's intent. If, for example, an author's purpose is to inform, to instruct, and to familiarize readers with a difficult subject, their use of connotation may be helpful. However, it may also undermine credibility and confuse readers. An author who wants to create a credible, scholarly effect in their text would most likely use denotation, which emphasizes literal, factual meaning and examples.

Technical Language

Test takers and critical readers alike should be very aware of technical language used within informational text. **Technical language** refers to terminology that is specific to a particular industry and is best understood by those specializing in that industry. This language is fairly easy to differentiate, since it will most likely be unfamiliar to readers. It's critical to be able to define technical language either by the author's written definition, through the use of an included glossary—if offered—or through context clues that help readers clarify word meaning.

Identifying Rhetorical Strategies

Rhetoric refers to an author's use of particular strategies, appeals, and devices to persuade an intended audience. The more effective the use of rhetoric, the more likely the audience will be persuaded.

Determining an Author's Point of View

A **rhetorical strategy**—also referred to as a rhetorical mode—is the structural way an author chooses to present their argument.

The following are some of the more common rhetorical strategies:

- *Cause and effect*—establishing a logical correlation or causation between two ideas

- *Classification/division*—the grouping of similar items together or division of something into parts

- *Comparison/contrast*—the distinguishing of similarities/differences to expand on an idea

- *Definition*—used to clarify abstract ideas, unfamiliar concepts, or to distinguish one idea from another

- *Description*—use of vivid imagery, active verbs, and clear adjectives to explain ideas

- *Exemplification*—the use of examples to explain an idea

- *Narration*—anecdotes or personal experience to present or expand on a concept

20

- *Problem/Solution*—presentation of a problem or problems, followed by proposed solution(s)

Rhetorical Strategies and Devices

A **rhetorical device** is the phrasing and presentation of an idea that reinforces and emphasizes a point in an argument. A rhetorical device is often quite memorable. One of the more famous uses of a rhetorical device is in John F. Kennedy's 1961 inaugural address: "Ask not what your country can do for you, ask what you can do for your country." The contrast of ideas presented in the phrasing is an example of the rhetorical device of antimetabole.

Some other common examples are provided below, but test takers should be aware that this is not a complete list.

Device	Definition	Example
Allusion	A reference to a famous person, event, or significant literary text as a form of significant comparison	"We are apt to shut our eyes against a painful truth, and listen to the song of that siren till she transforms us into beasts." Patrick Henry
Anaphora	The repetition of the same words at the beginning of successive words, phrases, or clauses, designed to emphasize an idea	"We shall not flag or fail. We shall go on to the end. We shall fight in France, we shall fight on the seas and oceans, we shall fight with growing confidence ... we shall fight in the fields and in the streets, we shall fight in the hills. We shall never surrender." Winston Churchill
Understatement	A statement meant to portray a situation as less important than it actually is to create an ironic effect	"The war in the Pacific has not necessarily developed in Japan's favor." Emperor Hirohito, surrendering Japan in World War II
Parallelism	A syntactical similarity in a structure or series of structures used for impact of an idea, making it memorable	"A penny saved is a penny earned." Ben Franklin
Rhetorical question	A question posed that is not answered by the writer though there is a desired response, most often designed to emphasize a point	"Can anyone look at our reduced standing in the world today and say, 'Let's have four more years of this?'" Ronald Reagan

Literature refers to a collection of written works that are the distinctive voices of peoples, time periods, and cultures. The world has gained great insight into human thought, vices, virtues, and desires through the written word. As the work pertains to the author's approach to these insights, literature can be classified as fiction or non-fiction.

Understanding the Characteristics of Literary Genres

Classifying literature involves an understanding of the concept of genre. A *genre* is a category of literature that possesses similarities in style and in characteristics. Based on form and structure, there are four basic genres.

Fictional Prose

Fictional prose consists of fictional works written in standard form with a natural flow of speech and without poetic structure. Fictional prose primarily utilizes grammatically complete sentences and a paragraph structure to convey its message.

Drama

Drama is fiction that is written to be performed in a variety of media, intended to be performed for an audience, and structured for that purpose. It might be composed using poetry or prose, often straddling the elements of both in what actors are expected to present. Action and dialogue are the tools used in drama to tell the story.

Poetry

Poetry is fiction in verse that has a unique focus on the rhythm of language and focuses on intensity of feeling. It is not an entire story, though it may tell one; it is compact in form and in function. Poetry can be considered as a poet's brief word picture for a reader. Poetic structure is primarily composed of lines and stanzas. Together, poetic structure and devices are the methods that poets use to lead readers to feeling an effect and, ultimately, to the interpretive message.

Literary Nonfiction

Literary nonfiction is prose writing that is based on current or past real events or real people and includes straightforward accounts as well as those that offer opinions on facts or factual events. It is helpful to distinguish between literary nonfiction—a form of writing that incorporates literary styles and techniques to create factually-based narratives—and informational texts, which will be addressed in the next section.

Informational Texts

Informational texts are a category of texts within the genre of nonfiction. Their intent is to inform, and while they do convey a point of view and may include literary devices, they do not utilize other literary elements, such as characters or plot. An informational text also reflects a thesis—an implicit or explicit statement of the text's intent and/or a main idea—the overarching focus and/or purpose of the text, generally implied. Some examples of informational texts are informative articles, instructional/how-to texts, factual reports, reference texts, and self-help texts.

Interpreting Textual Evidence in Informational Text

Literal and Figurative Meanings

It is important when evaluating informational texts to consider the use of both literal and figurative meanings. The words and phrases an author chooses to include in a text must be evaluated. How does the word choice affect the meaning and tone? By recognizing the use of literal and figurative language, a reader can more readily ascertain the message or purpose of a text. Literal word choice is the easiest to analyze as it represents the usual and intended way a word or phrase is used. It is also more common in informational texts because it is used to state facts and definitions. While figurative language is typically associated with fiction and poetry, it can be found in informational texts as well. The reader must determine not only what is meant by the figurative language in context, but also how the author intended it to shape the overall text.

Inference in Informational Text

Inference refers to the reader's ability to understand the unwritten text, i.e., "read between the lines" in terms of an author's intent or message. The strategy asks that a reader not take everything he or she reads at face value but instead, add their own interpretation of what the author seems to be trying to convey. A reader's ability to make inferences relies on their ability to think clearly and logically about the text. It does not ask that the reader make wild speculation or guess about the material but demands that he or she be able to come to a sound conclusion about the material.

An author's use of less literal words and phrases requires readers to make more inference when they read. Since inference involves deduction—deriving conclusions from ideas assumed to be true—there's more room for interpretation. Still, critical readers who employ inference, if careful in their thinking, can still arrive at the logical, sound conclusions the author intends.

Textual Evidence in Informational Text

Once a reader has determined an author's thesis or main idea, he or she will need to understand how textual evidence supports interpretation of that thesis or main idea. Test takers will be asked direct questions regarding an author's main idea and may be asked to identify evidence that would support those ideas. This will require test takers to comprehend literal and figurative meanings within the text passage, be able to draw inferences from provided information, and be able to separate important evidence from minor supporting detail. It's often helpful to skim test questions and answer options prior to critically reading informational text; however, test takers should avoid the temptation to solely look for the correct answers. Just trying to find the "right answer" may cause test takers to miss important supporting textual evidence. Making mental note of test questions is only helpful as a guide when reading.

After identifying an author's thesis or main idea, a test taker should look at the supporting details that the author provides to back up their assertions, identifying those additional pieces of information that help expand the thesis. From there, test takers should examine the additional information and related details for credibility, the author's use of outside sources, and be able to point to direct evidence that supports the author's claims. It's also imperative that test takers be able to identify what is strong support and what is merely additional information that is nice to know but not necessary. Being able to make this differentiation will help test takers effectively answer questions regarding an author's use of supporting evidence within informational text.

23

Understanding Organizational Patterns and Structures

Organizational Structure within Informational Text

Informational text is specifically designed to relate factual information, and although it is open to a reader's interpretation and application of the facts, the structure of the presentation is carefully designed to lead the reader to a particular conclusion or central idea. When reading informational text, it is important that readers are able to understand its organizational structure as the structure often directly relates to an author's intent to inform and/or persuade the reader.

The first step in identifying the text's structure is to determine the thesis or main idea. The thesis statement and organization of a work are closely intertwined. A thesis statement indicates the writer's purpose and may include the scope and direction of the text. It may be presented at the beginning of a text or at the end, and it may be explicit or implicit.

Once a reader has a grasp of the thesis or main idea of the text, he or she can better determine its organizational structure. Test takers are advised to read informational text passages more than once in order to comprehend the material fully. It is also helpful to examine any text features present in the text including the table of contents, index, glossary, headings, footnotes, and visuals. The analysis of these features and the information presented within them, can offer additional clues about the central idea and structure of a text. The following questions should be asked when considering structure:

- How does the author assemble the parts to make an effective whole argument?

- Is the passage linear in nature and if so, what is the timeline or thread of logic?

- What is the presented order of events, facts, or arguments? Are these effective in contributing to the author's thesis?

- How can the passage be divided into sections? How are they related to each other and to the main idea or thesis?

- What key terms are used to indicate the organization?

Next, test takers should skim the passage, noting the first line or two of each body paragraph—the **topic sentences**—and the conclusion. Key **transitional terms**, such as on the other hand, also, because, however, therefore, most importantly, and first, within the text can also signal organizational structure. Based on these clues, readers should then be able to identify what type of organizational structure is being used. The following organizational structures are most common:

- *Problem/solution*—organized by an analysis/overview of a problem, followed by potential solution(s)

- *Cause/effect*—organized by the effects resulting from a cause or the cause(s) of a particular effect

- *Spatial order*—organized by points that suggest location or direction—e.g., top to bottom, right to left, outside to inside

- *Chronological/sequence order*—organized by points presented to indicate a passage of time or through purposeful steps/stages

24

- *Comparison/Contrast*—organized by points that indicate similarities and/or differences between two things or concepts

- *Order of importance*—organized by priority of points, often most significant to least significant or vice versa

Workplace and Community Documents

Workplace and community documents help employers to communicate within the business world and foster positive community relations outside of it. Workplace communications typically craft a specific message to a targeted audience while community documents send a broader or more generic message to a wider range of recipients.

Workplace Documents

Even though workplace-related documents are generated in a multitude of paper and electronic formats—memorandums, bulletin boards, presentations, web conferencing, instant messaging, and e-mails—in general all effective business communications share relevant information concisely, accurately, and purposefully. Supervisors rely on workplace documents to communicate expectations to subordinates (downward communication), and subordinates rely on workplace documents to submit progress reports, ask questions, and address concerns with their supervisors (upward communication).

- Memorandums: Designed to communicate information to a wide audience, memorandums inform staff of company-wide policy changes. Similar to an e-mail, a memorandum has a header near the top which identifies the intended audience, the author of the memo, the subject of the memo, and the date it was issued. Unlike an e-mail, though, memorandums are longer, can be submitted in paper or electronic form, and contain an introduction that identifies the topic or problem, a body that expands on the topic, and a conclusion that suggests a course of action or solution.

- Bulletin Boards: Regardless of whether they are in paper or electronic form, bulletin boards provide a less formal setting for supervisors and staff to communicate. Bulletin boards are a perfect medium to post federal and state regulations, employee incentive initiatives, volunteer opportunities, and company news. While paper bulletin boards are limited to a specific office and personnel, electronic bulletin boards have the capability of broadcasting information nationally and even globally.

- Presentations: Presentations can be created with a variety of software—*PowerPoints*, *Google Slides*, and *Prezi*—and are given extemporaneously. Typically, presentations have an introductory slide, informational slides, and a concluding slide that gives the presenter's audience the opportunity to ask questions or create a dialogue. Presentations relay information in a media-rich format: graphics, tables, and hyperlinked documents and videos are easily imbedded within the slides.

- Web Conferencing: Web conferencing allows for employees to collaborate on projects and tasks. Employees are able to talk or videoconference from different locations, making it possible for remote workers from around the globe to participate simultaneously in one meeting. Web conferencing can be done via telephone with visuals (*PowerPoint* or *Microsoft Word* documents) or via video camera programs like *WebEx®*, *PGI GlobalMeet®*, and *Skype®*.

25

- Instant Messaging: Many staff outside of centralized locations who cannot communicate verbally with coworkers or supervisors rely, instead, on instant messaging programs. Instant messaging programs can deliver messages one-on-one or in circles and groups, and some software even provides screen-sharing capabilities. Since instant messaging is faster than e-mail, for many employees it has become the preferred method of communicating over long distances.

- E-Mails: In today's fast-paced business world, e-mails are heavily relied upon because they provide a platform that is perfect for quickly communicating brief, concise messages to targeted audiences. E-mails not only detail who the sender and receiver are but also provide a date, time, and subject line. Unlike a memorandum, sender and receiver can communicate back and forth, and, more importantly, they may do so over long distances. Many businesses today rely on *Google*, *Yahoo*, and *Outlook* mail severs.

Community Documents

Where business documents target a specific audience and often contain a higher level of proprietary, confidential, or sensitive information, community documents invite larger groups to discuss business matters in a less restrictive environment. Because community documents often help bridge the gap between businesses and community, an effective newsletter, discussion board, blog, website, and app have the power to influence public perception of private companies.

- Newsletters: Newsletters are used to provide the public information about the business. It can be used to generate excitement, inform or persuade staff or consumers, or give tips on how the public can contact or work with businesses. Newsletters can be mailed or sent electronically. Generally, newsletters are sent weekly, monthly, or quarterly. They can be interactive, providing the community a glance at what is going on with a business that they interact with, and, moreover, newsletters can communicate a company's mission, values, and priorities.

- Discussion Boards: Discussion boards offer a place to go to share information on a specific topic. Discussion boards are organized on menus, submenus, and discussion threads. People visit discussion boards to find out more about a topic. Discussion board members are granted greater access to the site and have greater power to publish and comment, but, still, visitors are welcome, and they often get difficult or obscure questions resolved.

- Blogs: A blog, which is usually centered on a specific topic or theme, is a website where individuals post and update information constantly. Blogs tend to feature the newest posts first while archiving older ones. Articles, editorials, images, videos, surveys, and social media (just to name a few) can all be imbedded within blogs. Menus, sidebars, recent posts, and search boxes help visitors wade through a dizzying array of media formats and topics. Though individuals can hire a web designer to create a blog for them, most people use existing platforms like *WordPress®*, *Blogger®*, and *Tumbler®*.

- Websites: As the world becomes more technologically savvy, a website can be used to house community documents, giving consumers instant access to tools they will need to interact with the business. It can house forms, contact information, discussion boards, surveys, and blogs. It is a one-stop-shop that can assist in the interaction between the business and the consumer. Websites are advantageous because they can be accessed via computer, tablet, or mobile phone.

- Apps: Similar to a website, an application (app) gives businesses yet another method to reach individuals or segments of a community. Apps provide instant access to forms and other documentation. Designed to be downloaded on tablets or mobile phones, apps are streamlined and intuitive, allowing consumers on the go to access information at their convenience. The primary operating systems for apps include *iOS®* and *Android®*.

Identifying Primary Sources in Media

Primary sources are best defined as records or items that serve as historical evidence. To be considered primary, the source documents or objects must have been created during the time period in which they reference. Examples include diaries, newspaper articles, speeches, government documents, photographs, and historical artifacts. In today's digital age, primary sources, which were once in print, often are embedded in secondary sources. Secondary sources, such as websites, history books, databases, or reviews, contain analysis or commentary on primary sources. **Secondary sources** borrow information from primary sources through the process of quoting, summarizing, or paraphrasing.

Today's students often complete research online through electronic sources. Electronic sources offer advantages over print and can be accessed on virtually any computer, while libraries or other research centers are limited to fixed locations and specific catalogs. Electronic sources are also efficient and yield massive amounts of data in seconds. The user can tailor a search based on key words, publication years, and article length. Lastly, many databases provide the user with instant citations, saving the user the trouble of manually assembling sources.

Though electronic sources yield powerful results, researchers must use caution. While there are many reputable and reliable sources on the internet, just as many are unreliable or biased sources. It's up to the researcher to examine and verify the reliability of sources. *Wikipedia*, for example, may or may not be accurate, depending on the contributor. Many databases, such as *EBSCO* or *SIRS*, offer peer reviewed articles, meaning the publications have been reviewed for the quality of their content.

Evaluating an Argument and its Claims

It's important to evaluate the author's supporting details to be sure that the details are credible, provide evidence of the author's point, and directly support the main idea. Though shocking statistics grab readers' attention, their use could be ineffective information in the piece. Details like this are crucial to understanding the passage and evaluating how well the author presents their argument and evidence.

Readers draw **conclusions** about what an author has presented. This helps them better understand what the writer has intended to communicate and whether or not they agree with what the author has offered. There are a few ways to determine a logical conclusion, but careful reading is the most important. It's helpful to read a passage a few times, noting details that seem important to the piece. Sometimes, readers arrive at a conclusion that is different than what the writer intended or come up with more than one conclusion.

Evidence

It is important to distinguish between *fact and opinion* when reading a piece of writing. When an author presents **facts**, such as statistics or data, readers should be able to check those facts and make sure they are accurate. When authors use **opinion**, they are sharing their own thoughts and feelings about a subject.

27

Textual evidence helps readers draw a conclusion about a passage. Textual evidence refers to information—facts and examples that support the main point; it will likely come from outside sources and can be in the form of quoted or paraphrased material. In order to draw a conclusion from evidence, it's important to examine the credibility and validity of that evidence as well as how (and if) it relates to the main idea.

Credibility

Critical readers examine the facts used to support an author's argument. They check the facts against other sources to be sure those facts are correct. They also check the validity of the sources used to be sure those sources are credible, academic, and/or peer-reviewed. Consider that when an author uses another person's opinion to support their argument, even if it is an expert's opinion, it is still only an opinion and should not be taken as fact. A strong argument uses valid, measurable facts to support ideas. Even then, the reader may disagree with the argument as it may be rooted in their personal beliefs.

An authoritative argument may use the facts to sway the reader. Because of this, a writer may choose to only use the information and expert opinion that supports their viewpoint.

Appeal to Emotion

An author's argument might also appeal to readers' emotions, perhaps by including personal stories and anecdotes (a short narrative of a specific event).

The next example presents an appeal to emotion. By sharing the personal anecdote of one student and speaking about emotional topics like family relationships, the author invokes the reader's empathy in asking them to reconsider the school rule.

> Our school should abolish its current ban on campus cell phone use. If students aren't able to use their phones during the school day, many of them feel isolated from their loved ones. For example, last semester, one student's grandmother had a heart attack in the morning. However, because he couldn't use his cell phone, the student didn't know about his grandmother's accident until the end of the day—when she had already passed away, and it was too late to say goodbye. By preventing students from contacting their friends and family, our school is placing undue stress and anxiety on students.

Counter-Arguments

If an author presents a differing opinion or a **counter-argument** in order to refute it, the reader should consider how and why the information is being presented. It is meant to strengthen the original argument and shouldn't be confused with the author's intended conclusion, but it should also be considered in the reader's final evaluation. On the contrary, sometimes authors will concede to an opposing argument by recognizing the validity the other side has to offer. A concession will allow readers to see both sides of the argument in an unbiased light, thereby increasing the credibility of the author.

Authors can also reflect **bias** if they ignore an opposing viewpoint or present their side in an unbalanced way. A strong argument considers the opposition and finds a way to refute it. Critical readers should look for an unfair or one-sided presentation of the argument and be skeptical, as a bias may be present.

Even if this bias is unintentional, if it exists in the writing, the reader should be wary of the validity of the argument.

Revising/Editing

Parts of Speech

Nouns

A noun is a person, place, thing, or idea. All nouns fit into one of two types, common or proper.

A common noun is a word that identifies any of a class of people, places, or things. Examples include numbers, objects, animals, feelings, concepts, qualities, and actions. *A, an,* or *the* usually precedes the common noun. These parts of speech are called articles. Here are some examples of sentences using nouns preceded by articles.

> *A* building is under construction.
> *The* girl would like to move to *the* city.

A proper noun (also called a proper name) is used for the specific name of an individual person, place, or organization. The first letter in a proper noun is capitalized. "My name is *Mary*." "I work for *Walmart*."

Nouns sometimes serve as adjectives (which themselves describe nouns), such as "hockey player" and "state government."

Pronouns

A word used in place of a noun is known as a pronoun. Pronouns are words like *I, mine, hers,* and *us*.

Pronouns can be split into different classifications (seen below) which make them easier to learn; however, it's not important to memorize the classifications.

- Personal pronouns: refer to people places, things, etc.
- First person: we, I, our, mine
- Second person: you, yours
- Third person: he, them
- Possessive pronouns: demonstrate ownership (mine, his, hers, its, ours, theirs, yours)
- Interrogative pronouns: ask questions (what, which, who, whom, whose)
- Relative pronouns: include the five interrogative pronouns and others that are relative (whoever, whomever, that, when, where)
- Demonstrative pronouns: replace something specific (this, that, those, these)
- Reciprocal pronouns: indicate something was done or given in return (each other, one another)
- Indefinite pronouns: have a nonspecific status (anybody, whoever, someone, everybody, somebody)

Indefinite pronouns such as *anybody, whoever, someone, everybody*, and *somebody* command a singular verb form, but others such as *all, none,* and *some* could require a singular or plural verb form.

Antecedents

An antecedent is the noun to which a pronoun refers; it needs to be written or spoken before the pronoun is used. For many pronouns, antecedents are imperative for clarity. In particular, a lot of the personal, possessive, and demonstrative pronouns need antecedents. Otherwise, it would be unclear who or what someone is referring to when they use a pronoun like *he* or *this*.

Pronoun reference means that the pronoun should refer clearly to one, clear, unmistakable noun (the antecedent).

Pronoun-antecedent agreement refers to the need for the antecedent and the corresponding pronoun to agree in gender, person, and number. Here are some examples:

The *kidneys* (plural antecedent) are part of the urinary system. *They* (plural pronoun) serve several roles.

The kidneys are part of the *urinary system* (singular antecedent). *It* (singular pronoun) is also known as the renal system.

Pronoun Cases

The subjective pronouns —*I, you, he/she/it, we, they,* and *who*—are the subjects of the sentence.

Example: *They* have a new house.

The objective pronouns—*me, you* (*singular*), *him/her, us, them,* and *whom*—are used when something is being done for or given to someone; they are objects of the action.

Example: The teacher has an apple for *us*.

The possessive pronouns—*mine, my, your, yours, his, hers, its, their, theirs, our,* and *ours*—are used to denote that something (or someone) belongs to someone (or something).

Example: It's *their* chocolate cake.
Even Better Example: It's *my* chocolate cake!

One of the greatest challenges and worst abuses of pronouns concerns *who* and *whom*. Just knowing the following rule can eliminate confusion. *Who* is a subjective-case pronoun used only as a subject or subject complement. *Whom* is only objective-case and, therefore, the object of the verb or preposition.

Who is going to the concert?

You are going to the concert with *whom*?

Hint: When using *who* or *whom*, think of whether someone would say *he* or *him*. If the answer is *he*, use *who*. If the answer is *him*, use *whom*. This trick is easy to remember because *he* and *who* both end in vowels, and *him* and *whom* both end in the letter *M*.

Adjectives

"The *extraordinary* brain is the *main* organ of the central nervous system." The adjective *extraordinary* describes the brain in a way that causes one to realize it is more exceptional than some of the other organs while the adjective *main* defines the brain's importance in its system.

An *adjective* is a word or phrase that names an attribute that describes or clarifies a noun or pronoun. This helps the reader visualize and understand the characteristics—size, shape, age, color, origin, etc.—of a person, place, or thing that otherwise might not be known. Adjectives breathe life, color, and depth into the subjects they define.

Adjectives often precede the nouns they describe.

> *She drove her <u>new</u> car.*

However, adjectives can also come later in the sentence.

> *Her car is <u>new</u>.*

Adjectives using the prefix *a*– can only be used after a verb.

> Correct: The dog was alive until the car ran up on the curb and hit him.
> Incorrect: The alive dog was hit by a car that ran up on the curb.

Other examples of this rule include *awake, ablaze, ajar, alike,* and *asleep.*

Other adjectives used after verbs concern states of health.

> The girl was finally *well* after a long bout of pneumonia.
> The boy was *fine* after the accident.

An adjective phrase is not a bunch of adjectives strung together, but a group of words that describes a noun or pronoun and, thus, functions as an adjective. Very happy is an adjective phrase; so are way too hungry and passionate about traveling.

Possessives

In grammar, **possessive nouns** and **possessive pronouns** show ownership.

Singular nouns are generally made possessive with an apostrophe and an *s* (*'s*).

> My *uncle's* new car is silver.
> The *dog's* bowl is empty.
> *James's* ties are becoming outdated.

Plural nouns ending in *s* are generally made possessive by just adding an apostrophe ('):

> The pistachio nuts' saltiness is added during roasting. (The saltiness of pistachio nuts is added during roasting.)

> The students' achievement tests are difficult. (The achievement tests of the students are difficult.)

If the plural noun does not end in an *s* such as *women,* then it is made possessive by adding an apostrophe *s* (*'s*)—*women's.*

Possessive pronouns can be first person (*mine*), second person (*yours*), or third person (*theirs*).

31

Indefinite possessive pronouns such as *nobody* or *someone* become possessive by adding an *apostrophe s* to become *nobody's* or *someone's*.

Verbs

A verb is the part of speech that describes an action, state of being, or occurrence.

A verb forms the main part of a predicate of a sentence. This means that the verb explains what the noun (which will be discussed shortly) is doing. A simple example is *time <u>flies</u>*. The verb *flies* explains what the action of the noun, *time*, is doing. This example is a *main* verb.

Helping (auxiliary) verbs are words like *have, do, be, can, may, should, must,* and *will.* "I *should* go to the store." Helping verbs assist main verbs in expressing tense, ability, possibility, permission, or obligation.

Particles are minor function words like *not, in, out, up,* or *down* that become part of the verb itself. "I might *not*."

Participles are words formed from verbs that are often used to modify a noun, noun phrase, verb, or verb phrase.

The *running* teenager collided with the cyclist.

Participles can also create compound verb forms.

He is *speaking*.

Verbs have five basic forms: the *base* form, the *-s* form, the *-ing* form, the *past* form, and the *past participle* form.

The past forms are either regular (*love/loved; hate/hated*) or irregular because they don't end by adding the common past tense suffix "-ed" (*go/went; fall/fell; set/set*).

Adverbs

Adverbs have more functions than adjectives because they modify or qualify verbs, adjectives, or other adverbs as well as word groups that express a relation of place, time, circumstance, or cause. Therefore, adverbs answer any of the following questions: *How, when, where, why, in what way, how often, how much, in what condition,* and/or *to what degree. How good looking is he? He is <u>very</u> handsome.*

Here are some examples of adverbs for different situations:

- how: quickly
- when: daily
- where: there
- in what way: easily
- how often: often
- how much: much
- in what condition: badly
- what degree: hardly

As one can see, for some reason, many adverbs end in *-ly.*

Adverbs do things like emphasize (*really, simply,* and *so*), amplify (*heartily, completely,* and *positively*), and tone down (*almost, somewhat,* and *mildly*).

Adverbs also come in phrases.

> The dog ran as <u>though his life depended on it.</u>

Prepositions

Prepositions are connecting words and, while there are only about 150 of them, they are used more often than any other individual groups of words. They describe relationships between other words. They are placed before a noun or pronoun, forming a phrase that modifies another word in the sentence. Prepositional phrases begin with a preposition and end with a noun or pronoun, the object of the preposition. *A pristine lake is <u>near the store</u> and <u>behind the bank</u>.*

Some commonly used prepositions are *about, after, anti, around, as, at, behind, beside, by, for, from, in, into, of, off, on, to,* and *with.*

Complex prepositions, which also come before a noun or pronoun, consist of two or three words such as *according to, in regards to,* and *because of.*

Interjections

Interjections are words used to express emotion. Examples include *wow, ouch,* and *hooray*. Interjections are often separate from sentences; in those cases, the interjection is directly followed by an exclamation point. In other cases, the interjection is included in a sentence and followed by a comma. The punctuation plays a big role in the intensity of the emotion that the interjection is expressing. Using a comma or semicolon indicates less excitement than using an exclamation mark.

Conjunctions

Conjunctions are vital words that connect words, phrases, thoughts, and ideas. Conjunctions show relationships between components. There are two types:

Coordinating conjunctions are the primary class of conjunctions placed between words, phrases, clauses, and sentences that are of equal grammatical rank; the coordinating conjunctions are *for, and, nor, but, or, yet,* and *so*. A useful memorization trick is to remember that the first letter of these conjunctions collectively spell the word *fanboys*.

> I need to go shopping, *but* I must be careful to leave enough money in the bank.
> She wore a black, red, *and* white shirt.

Subordinating conjunctions are the secondary class of conjunctions. They connect two unequal parts, one main (or independent) and the other subordinate (or dependent). I must go to the store *even though* I do not have enough money in the bank.

> *Because* I read the review, I do not want to go to the movie.

Notice that the presence of subordinating conjunctions makes clauses dependent. *I read the review* is an independent clause, but *because* makes the clause dependent. Thus, it needs an independent clause to complete the sentence.

Punctuation

Periods (.) are used to end a sentence that is a statement (declarative) or a command (imperative). They should not be used in a sentence that asks a question or is an exclamation. Periods are also used in abbreviations, which are shortened versions of words.

- Declarative: The boys refused to go to sleep.
- Imperative: Walk down to the bus stop.
- Abbreviations: Joan Roberts, M.D., Apple Inc., Mrs. Adamson
- If a sentence ends with an abbreviation, it is inappropriate to use two periods. It should end with a single period after the abbreviation.

The chef gathered the ingredients for the pie, which included apples, flour, sugar, etc.

Question marks *(?)* are used with direct questions (interrogative). An indirect question can use a period:

Interrogative: When does the next bus arrive?

Indirect Question: I wonder when the next bus arrives.

An exclamation point *(!)* is used to show strong emotion or can be used as an interjection. This punctuation should be used sparingly in formal writing situations.

What an amazing shot!

Whoa!

In a sentence, colons are used before a list, a summary or elaboration, or an explanation related to the preceding information in the sentence:

There are two ways to reserve tickets for the performance: by phone or in person.

One thing is clear: students are spending more on tuition than ever before.

As these examples show, a colon must be preceded by an independent clause. However, the information after the colon may be in the form of an independent clause or in the form of a list.

Semicolons can be used in two different ways—to join ideas or to separate them. In some cases, semicolons can be used to connect what would otherwise be stand-alone sentences. Each part of the sentence joined by a semicolon must be an independent clause. The use of a semicolon indicates that these two independent clauses are closely related to each other:

The rising cost of childcare is one major stressor for parents; healthcare expenses are another source of anxiety.

Classes have been canceled due to the snowstorm; check the school website for updates.

Semicolons can also be used to divide elements of a sentence in a more distinct way than simply using a comma. This usage is particularly useful when the items in a list are especially long and complex and contain other internal punctuation.

> Retirees have many modes of income: some survive solely off their retirement checks; others supplement their income through part time jobs, like working in a supermarket or substitute teaching; and others are financially dependent on the support of family members, friends, and spouses.

Subject-Verb Agreement

The subject of a sentence and its verb must agree. The cornerstone rule of subject-verb agreement is that subject and verb must agree in number. Whether the subject is singular or plural, the verb must follow suit.

> Incorrect: The houses is new.
> Correct: The houses are new.
> Also Correct: The house is new.

In other words, a singular subject requires a singular verb; a plural subject requires a plural verb. The words or phrases that come between the subject and verb do not alter this rule.

> Incorrect: The houses built of brick is new.
> Correct: The houses built of brick are new.

> Incorrect: The houses with the sturdy porches is new.
> Correct: The houses with the sturdy porches are new.

The subject will always follow the verb when a sentence begins with *here* or *there.* Identify these with care.

> Incorrect: Here *is* the *houses* with sturdy porches.
> Correct: Here *are* the *houses* with sturdy porches.

The subject in the sentences above is not *here*, it is *houses*. Remember, *here* and *there* are never subjects. Be careful that contractions such as *here's* or *there're* do not cause confusion!

Two subjects joined by *and* require a plural verb form, except when the two combine to make one thing:

> Incorrect: Garrett and Jonathan is over there.
> Correct: Garrett and Jonathan are over there.

> Incorrect: Spaghetti and meatballs are a delicious meal!
> Correct: Spaghetti and meatballs is a delicious meal!

In the example above, *spaghetti and meatballs* is a compound noun. However, *Garrett and Jonathan* is not a compound noun.

Two singular subjects joined by *or, either/or,* or *neither/nor* call for a singular verb form.

> Incorrect: Butter or syrup are acceptable.
> Correct: Butter or syrup is acceptable.

Plural subjects joined by *or, either/or,* or *neither/nor* are, indeed, plural.

> The chairs or the boxes are being moved next.

If one subject is singular and the other is plural, the verb should agree with the closest noun.

> Correct: The chair or the boxes are being moved next.
> Correct: The chairs or the box is being moved next.

Some plurals of money, distance, and time call for a singular verb.

> Incorrect: Three dollars *are* enough to buy that.
> Correct: Three dollars *is* enough to buy that.

For words declaring degrees of quantity such as *many of, some of,* or *most of,* let the noun that follows *of* be the guide:

> Incorrect: Many of the books is in the shelf.
> Correct: Many of the books are in the shelf.

> Incorrect: Most of the pie *are* on the table.
> Correct: Most of the pie *is* on the table.

For indefinite pronouns like anybody or everybody, use singular verbs.

> Everybody *is* going to the store.

However, the pronouns *few, many, several, all, some,* and *both* have their own rules and use plural forms.

> Some *are* ready.

Some nouns like *crowd* and *congress* are called collective nouns, and they require a singular verb form.

> Congress *is* in session.
> The news *is* over.

Books and movie titles, though, including plural nouns such as *Great Expectations*, also require a singular verb. Remember that only the subject affects the verb. While writing tricky subject-verb arrangements, say them aloud. Listen to them. Once the rules have been learned, one's ear will become sensitive to them, making it easier to pick out what's right and what's wrong.

Independent and Dependent Clauses

Independent and dependent clauses are strings of words that contain both a subject and a verb. An independent clause can stand alone as complete thought, but a dependent clause cannot. A dependent clause relies on other words to be a complete sentence.

Independent clause: The keys are on the counter.
Dependent clause: If the keys are on the counter

Notice that both clauses have a subject (*keys*) and a verb (*are*). The independent clause expresses a complete thought, but the word *if* at the beginning of the dependent clause makes it dependent on other words to be a complete thought.

Independent clause: If the keys are on the counter, please give them to me.

This example constitutes a complete sentence since it includes at least one verb and one subject and is a complete thought. In this case, the independent clause has two subjects (*keys* & an implied *you*) and two verbs (*are* & *give*).

Independent clause: I went to the store.
Dependent clause: Because we are out of milk,

Complete Sentence: Because we are out of milk, I went to the store.
Complete Sentence: I went to the store because we are out of milk.

A phrase is a group of words that does not contain both a subject and a verb.

Word Usage

Word usage: the way and manner in which writers choose to use words (or phrases). This is a vital consideration in order to create excellence in writing. Context plays a role in the selection of words, as does simple choice.

Correct word usage can be as basic and imperative as making the right grammatical choice.

Incorrect: I never *seen* that play
Correct: I never *saw* that play.

Seen (past participle of *see*) in place of *saw* (the correct past tense of *see*) is a relatively common and grievous mistake.

Incorrect: *There* going to the store with *there* parents.
Correct: *They're* going to the store with *their* parents.

There (adverb) mistaken for *they're* (contraction for "they are") and *there* (adverb) for *their* (pronoun) are also frequent grammatical errors.

Correct word usage can be as simple as choosing between synonyms. For instance, determining whether to say *for instance* or *for example*! Would it be better to use the word *incongruous* or *inappropriate* for *unsuited,* or when the woman is *uncouth,* would *redneck, uninformed,* or *illiterate* better define her?

Correct word usage can also be as simple as knowing how to access and make good use of dictionaries, thesauruses, grammar correction software, and search engines on computers, tablets, and smartphones.

Context Clues

Context clues help readers understand unfamiliar words, and thankfully, there are many types.

Synonyms are words or phrases that have nearly, if not exactly, the same meaning as other words or phrases

> *Large* boxes are needed to pack *big* items.

Antonyms are words or phrases that have opposite definitions. Antonyms, like synonyms, can serve as context clues, although more cryptically.

> *Large* boxes are not needed to pack *small* items.

Definitions are sometimes included within a sentence to define uncommon words.

> They practiced the *rumba*, a *type of dance*, for hours on end.

Explanations provide context through elaboration.

> Large boxes holding items weighing over 60 pounds were stacked in the corner.

Contrast provides ways in which things are different.

These *minute* creatures were much different than the *huge* mammals that the zoologist was accustomed to dealing with.

Word Parts

By analyzing and understanding Latin, Greek, and Anglo-Saxon word roots, prefixes, and suffixes one can better understand word meanings. Of course, people can always look words up if a dictionary or thesaurus, if available, but meaning can often be gleaned on the spot if the writer learns to dissect and examine words.

A word can consist of the following:

- root
- root + suffix
- prefix + root
- prefix + root + suffix

For example, if someone was unfamiliar with the word *submarine* they could break the word into its parts.

> prefix + root
> sub + marine

38

It can be determined that *sub* means *below* as in *subway* and *subpar*. Additionally, one can determine that *marine* refers to *the sea* as in *marine life*. Thus, it can be figured that *submarine* refers to something below the water.

Roots

Roots are the basic components of words. Many roots can stand alone as individual words, but others must be combined with a prefix or suffix to be a word. For example, *calc* is a root but it needs a suffix to be an actual word (*calcium*).

Prefixes

A *prefix* is a word, letter, or number that is placed before another. It adjusts or qualifies the root word's meaning. When written alone, prefixes are followed by a dash to indicate that the root word follows. Some of the most common prefixes are the following:

Prefix	Meaning	Example
dis-	not or opposite of	disabled
in-, im-, il-, ir-	not	illiterate
re-	again	return
un-	not	unpredictable
anti-	against	antibacterial
fore-	before	forefront
mis-	wrongly	misunderstand
non-	not	nonsense
over-	more than normal	overabundance
pre-	before	preheat
super-	above	superman

Suffixes

A suffix is a letter or group of letters added at the end of a word to form another word. The word created from the root and suffix is either a different tense of the same root (*help* + *ed* = *helped*) or a new word (*help* + *ful* = *helpful*). When written alone, suffixes are preceded by a dash to indicate that the root word comes before.

Some of the most common suffixes are the following:

Suffix	Meaning	Example
ed	makes a verb past tense	wash*ed*
ing	makes a verb a present participle verb	wash*ing*
ly	to make characteristic of	love*ly*
s/es	to make more than one	chair*s*, box*es*
able	can be done	deplor*able*
al	having characteristics of	comic*al*
est	comparative	great*est*
ful	full of	wonder*ful*
ism	belief in	commun*ism*
less	without	faith*less*
ment	action or process	accomplish*ment*
ness	state of	happi*ness*
ize, ise	to render, to make	steri*lize*, adver*tise*
cede/ceed/sede	go	con*cede*, pro*ceed*, super*sede*

Here are some helpful tips:

- When adding a suffix that starts with a vowel (for example, -*ed*) to a one-syllable root whose vowel has a short sound and ends in a consonant (for example, *stun*), double the final consonant of the root (*n*).

   stun + ed = stun*n*ed

   Exception: If the past tense verb ends in *x* such as *box*, do not double the *x*.

   box + ed = boxed

- If adding a suffix that starts with a vowel (-*er*) to a multi-syllable word ending in a consonant (*begin*), double the consonant (*n*).

   begin + er = begin*n*er

- If a short vowel is followed by two or more consonants in a word such as *i+t+c+h = itch*, do <u>not</u> double the last consonant.

   itch + ed = itched

- If adding a suffix that starts with a vowel (-*ing*) to a word ending in *e* (for example, *name*), that word's final *e* is generally (but not always) dropped.

   name + ing = naming
   exception: manage + able = manag*e*able

- If adding a suffix that starts with a consonant (*-ness*) to a word ending in *e* (*complete*), the *e* generally (but not always) remains.

> complete + ness = completeness
> exception: judge + ment = judgment

- There is great diversity on handling words that end in y. For words ending in a vowel + y, nothing changes in the original word.

> play + ed = played

- For words ending in a consonant + *y*, change the *y* to *i* when adding any suffix except for *–ing*.

> marry + ed = married
> marry + ing = marrying

Sentence Fluency

It's time to take what's been studied and put it all together in order to construct well-written sentences and paragraphs that have correct structure. Learning and utilizing the mechanics of structure will encourage effective, professional results, and adding some creativity will elevate one's writing to a higher level.

First, let's review the basic elements of sentences.

A sentence is a set of words that make up a grammatical unit. The words must have certain elements and be spoken or written in a specific order to constitute a complete sentence that makes sense.

> 1. A sentence must have a subject (a noun or noun phrase). The subject tells whom or what the sentence is addressing (i.e., what it is about).

> 2. A sentence must have an action or state of being (*a verb*). To reiterate: A verb forms the main part of the predicate of a sentence. This means that it explains what the noun is doing.

> 3. A sentence must convey a complete thought.

When examining writing, be mindful of grammar, structure, spelling, and patterns. Sentences can come in varying sizes and shapes; so, the point of grammatical correctness is not to stamp out creativity or diversity in writing. Rather, grammatical correctness ensures that writing will be enjoyable and clear. One of the most common methods for catching errors is to mouth the words as you read them. Many typos are fixed automatically by our brain, but mouthing the words often circumvents this instinct and helps one read what's actually on the page. Often, grammar errors are caught not by memorization of grammar rules but by the training of one's mind to know whether something sounds right or not.

A sentence fragment is a failed attempt to create a complete sentence because it's missing a required noun or verb. Fragments don't function properly because there isn't enough information to understand the writer's intended meaning. For example:

> Seat belt use corresponds to a lower rate of hospital visits, reducing strain on an already overburdened healthcare system. Insurance claims as well.

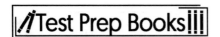

Look at the last sentence: *Insurance claims as well*. What does this mean? This is a fragment because it has a noun but no verb, and it leaves the reader guessing what the writer means about insurance claims. Many readers can probably infer what the writer means, but this distracts them from the flow of the writer's argument. Choosing a suitable replacement for a sentence fragment may be one of the questions on the test. The fragment is probably related to the surrounding content, so look at the overall point the writer is trying to make and choose the answer that best fits that idea.

Remember that sometimes a fragment can look like a complete sentence or have all the nouns and verbs it needs to make sense. Consider the following two examples:

Seat belt use corresponds to a lower rate of hospital visits.

Although seat belt use corresponds to a lower rate of hospital visits.

Both examples above have nouns and verbs, but only the first sentence is correct. The second sentence is a fragment, even though it's actually longer. The key is the writer's use of the word *although*. Starting a sentence with although turns that part into a subordinate clause (more on that next). Keep in mind that one doesn't have to remember that it's called a subordinate clause on the test. Just be able to recognize that the words form an incomplete thought and identify the problem as a sentence fragment.

A run-on sentence is, in some ways, the opposite of a fragment. It contains two or more sentences that have been improperly forced together into one. An example of a run-on sentence looks something like this:

Seat belt use corresponds to a lower rate of hospital visits it also leads to fewer insurance claims.

Here, there are two separate ideas in one sentence. It's difficult for the reader to follow the writer's thinking because there is no transition from one idea to the next. On the test, choose the best way to correct the run-on sentence.

Here are two possibilities for the sentence above:

Seat belt use corresponds to a lower rate of hospital visits. It also leads to fewer insurance claims.

Seat belt use corresponds to a lower rate of hospital visits, but it also leads to fewer insurance claims.

Both solutions are grammatically correct, so which one is the best choice? That depends on the point that the writer is trying to make. Always read the surrounding text to determine what the writer wants to demonstrate, and choose the option that best supports that thought.

Another type of run-on occurs when writers use inappropriate punctuation:

This winter has been very cold, some farmers have suffered damage to their crops.

Though a comma has been added, this sentence is still not correct. When a comma alone is used to join two independent clauses, it is known as a comma splice. Without an appropriate conjunction, a comma cannot join two independent clauses by itself.

Types of Sentences

There isn't an overabundance of absolutes in grammar, but here is one: every sentence in the English language falls into one of four categories.

- Declarative: a simple statement that ends with a period

  The price of milk per gallon is the same as the price of gasoline.

- Imperative: a command, instruction, or request that ends with a period

  Buy milk when you stop to fill up your car with gas.

- Interrogative: a question that ends with a question mark

  Will you buy the milk?

- Exclamatory: a statement or command that expresses emotions like anger, urgency, or surprise and ends with an exclamation mark

  Buy the milk now!

Declarative sentences are the most common type, probably because they are comprised of the most general content, without any of the bells and whistles that the other three types contain. They are, simply, declarations or statements of any degree of seriousness, importance, or information.

Imperative sentences often seem to be missing a subject. The subject is there, though; it is just not visible or audible because it is implied. Look at the imperative example sentence.

  Buy the milk when you fill up your car with gas.

You is the implied subject, the one to whom the command is issued. This is sometimes called *the understood you* because it is understood that *you* is the subject of the sentence.

Interrogative sentences—those that ask questions—are defined as such from the idea of the word interrogation, the action of questions being asked of suspects by investigators. Although that is serious business, interrogative sentences apply to all kinds of questions.

To exclaim is at the root of exclamatory sentences. These are made with strong emotions behind them. The only technical difference between a declarative or imperative sentence and an exclamatory one is the exclamation mark at the end. The example declarative and imperative sentences can both become an exclamatory one simply by putting an exclamation mark at the end of the sentences.

  The price of milk per gallon is the same as the price of gasoline!
  Buy milk when you stop to fill up your car with gas!

After all, someone might be really excited by the price of gas or milk, or they could be mad at the person that will be buying the milk! However, as stated before, exclamation marks in abundance defeat their own purpose! After a while, they begin to cause fatigue! When used only for their intended purpose, they can have their expected and desired effect.

43

Parallel Structure in a Sentence

Parallel structure, also known as parallelism, refers to using the same grammatical form within a sentence. This is important in lists and for other components of sentences.

> Incorrect: At the recital, the boys and girls were dancing, singing, and played musical instruments.
> Correct: At the recital, the boys and girls were dancing, singing, and playing musical instruments.

Notice that in the second example, *played* is not in the same verb tense as the other verbs, nor is it compatible with the helping verb *were*. To test for parallel structure in lists, try reading each item as if it were the only item in the list.

> The boys and girls were dancing.
> The boys and girls were singing.
> The boys and girls were played musical instruments.

Suddenly, the error in the sentence becomes very clear. Here's another example:

> Incorrect: After the accident, I informed the police *that Mrs. Holmes backed* into my car, *that Mrs. Holmes got out* of her car to look at the damage, and *she was driving* off without leaving a note.

> Correct: After the accident, I informed the police *that Mrs. Holmes backed* into my car, *that Mrs. Holmes got out* of her car to look at the damage, and *that Mrs. Holmes drove off* without leaving a note.

> Correct: After the accident, I informed the police that Mrs. Holmes *backed* into my car, *got out* of her car to look at the damage, and *drove off* without leaving a note.

Note that there are two ways to fix the nonparallel structure of the first sentence. The key to parallelism is consistent structure.

Sentence Structures

A simple sentence has one independent clause.

> I am going to win.

A compound sentence has two independent clauses. A conjunction—*for, and, nor, but, or, yet, so*—links them together. Note that each of the independent clauses has a subject and a verb.

> I am going to win, but the odds are against me.

A complex sentence has one independent clause and one or more dependent clauses.

> I am going to win, even though I don't deserve it.

Even though I don't deserve it is a dependent clause. It does not stand on its own. Some conjunctions that link an independent and a dependent clause are *although, because, before, after, that, when, which*, and *while*.

44

A compound-complex sentence has at least three clauses, two of which are independent and at least one that is a dependent clause.

While trying to dance, I tripped over my partner's feet, but I regained my balance quickly.

The dependent clause is *While trying to dance*.

Forming Paragraphs

A good paragraph should have the following characteristics:

- Be logical with organized sentences
- Have a unified purpose within itself
- Use sentences as building blocks
- Be a distinct section of a piece of writing
- Present a single theme introduced by a topic sentence
- Maintain a consistent flow through subsequent, relevant, well-placed sentences
- Tell a story of its own or have its own purpose, yet connect with what is written before and after
- Enlighten, entertain, and/or inform

Though certainly not set in stone, the length should be a consideration for the reader's sake, not merely for the sake of the topic. When paragraphs are especially short, the reader might experience an irregular, uneven effect; when they're much longer than 250 words, the reader's attention span, and probably their retention, is challenged. While a paragraph can technically be a sentence long, a good rule of thumb is for paragraphs to be at least three sentences long and no more than ten sentence long. An optimal word length is 100 to 250 words.

Coherent Paragraphs

Coherence is simply defined as the quality of being logical and consistent. In order to have coherent paragraphs, therefore, authors must be logical and consistent in their writing, whatever the document might be. Two words are helpful to understanding coherence: flow and relationship. Earlier, transitions were referred to as being the "glue" to put organized thoughts together. Now, let's look at the topic sentence from which flow and relationship originate.

The topic sentence, usually the first in a paragraph, holds the essential features that will be brought forth in the paragraph. It is also here that authors either grab or lose readers. It may be the only writing that a reader encounters from that writer, so it is a good idea to summarize and represent ideas accurately.

The coherent paragraph has a logical order. It utilizes transitional words and phrases, parallel sentence structure, clear pronoun references, and reasonable repetition of key words and phrases. Use common sense for repetition. Consider synonyms for variety. Be consistent in verb tense whenever possible.

When writers have accomplished their paragraph's purpose, they prepare it to receive the next paragraph. While writing, read the paragraph over, edit, examine, evaluate, and make changes accordingly. Possibly, a paragraph has gone on too long. If that occurs, it needs to be broken up into other paragraphs, or the length should be reduced. If a paragraph didn't fully accomplish its purpose, consider revising it.

Transitions

Transitions are the glue used to make organized thoughts adhere to one another. Transitions help blend ideas together seamlessly, within sentences and paragraphs, between them, and (in longer documents) even between sections. Transitions may be single words, sentences, or whole paragraphs. Transitions help readers to digest and understand what to feel about what has gone on and clue readers in on what is going on, what will be, and how they might react to all these factors. Transitions are like good clues left at a crime scene.

Transitions have many emphases as can be seen below.

- To show emphasis: truly, in fact
- To show examples: for example, namely, specifically
- To show similarities: also, likewise
- To show dissimilarities: on the other hand, even if, in contrast
- To show progression of time: later, previously, subsequently
- To show sequence or order: next, finally
- To show cause and effect: therefore, so
- To show place or position: above, nearby, there
- To provide evidence: furthermore, then
- To summarize: finally, summarizing

Math

Numbers and Operations

Properties of Operations with Real Numbers

The mathematical number system is made up of two general types of numbers: real and complex. **Real numbers** are both irrational and rational numbers, while **complex numbers** are composed of both real number and an imaginary ones. Imaginary numbers are the result of taking the square root of -1, and $\sqrt{-1} = i$.

The real number system is often explained using a Venn diagram similar to the one below. After a number has been labeled as a real number, further classification occurs when considering the other groups in this diagram. If a number is a never-ending, non-repeating decimal, it falls in the irrational category. Otherwise, it is rational. Furthermore, if a number does not have a fractional part, it is classified as an integer, such as -2, 75, or zero. Whole numbers are an even smaller group that only includes positive integers and zero. The last group of natural numbers is made up of only positive integers, such as 2, 56, or 12.

Both positive and negative numbers are valued according to their distance from 0. Both +3 and -3 can be considered using the following number line:

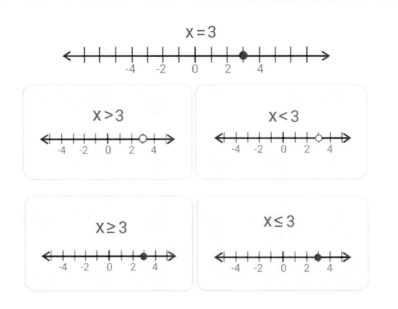

Both 3 and -3 are three spaces from 0. The distance from 0 is called its **absolute value**. Thus, both -3 and 3 have an absolute value of 3 since they're both three spaces away from 0.

An absolute number is written by placing | | around the number. So, |3| and |−3| both equal 3, as that's their common absolute value.

Real numbers can be compared and ordered using the number line. If a number falls to the left on the real number line, it is less than a number on the right. For example, $−2 < 5$ because -2 falls to the left of zero, and 5 falls to the right. Numbers to the left of zero are negative while those to the right are positive.

The order of operations—PEMDAS—simplifies longer expressions with real or imaginary numbers. Each operation is listed in the order of how they should be completed in a problem containing more than one operation. Parentheses can also mean grouping symbols, such as brackets and absolute value. Then, exponents are calculated. Multiplication and division should be completed from left to right, and addition and subtraction should be completed from left to right. The following shows step-by-step how an expression is simplified using the order of operations:

$$25 \div (8 − 3)^2 − 1$$

$$25 \div (5)^2 − 1$$

$$25 \div 25 − 1$$

$$1 − 1$$

$$0$$

48

Simplification of another type of expression occurs when radicals are involved. For example, the following expression is a radical, or root, that can be simplified: $\sqrt{24x^2}$. First, the number must be factored out to the highest perfect square. Any perfect square can be taken out of a radical. Twenty-four can be factored into 4 and 6, and 4 can be taken out of the radical. $\sqrt{4} = 2$ can be taken out, and 6 stays underneath. If $x > 0$, x can be taken out of the radical because it is a perfect square. The simplified radical is $2x\sqrt{6}$. An approximation can be found using a calculator.

There are also properties of numbers that are true for certain operations. The **commutative** property allows the order of the terms in an expression to change while keeping the same final answer. Both addition and multiplication can be completed in any order and still obtain the same result. However, order does matter in subtraction and division. The **associative** property allows any terms to be "associated" by parentheses and retain the same final answer. For example,

$$(4 + 3) + 5 = 4 + (3 + 5)$$

Both addition and multiplication are associative; however, subtraction and division do not hold this property. The **distributive** property states that $a(b + c) = ab + ac$. It is a property that involves both addition and multiplication, and the a is distributed onto each term inside the parentheses.

Integers can be factored into prime numbers. To **factor** is to express as a product. For example,

$$6 = 3 \times 2 \text{ and } 6 = 6 \times 1$$

Both are factorizations, but the expression involving the factors of 3 and 2 is known as a **prime factorization** because it is factored into a product of two **prime numbers**—integers which do not have any factors other than themselves and 1. A **composite number** is a positive integer that can be divided into at least one other integer other than itself and 1, such as 6. Integers that have a factor of 2 are even, and if they are not divisible by 2, they are odd. Finally, a **multiple** of a number is the product of that number and a counting number—also known as a **natural number**. For example, some multiples of 4 are 4, 8, 12, 16, etc.

The **greatest common factor** is the largest number among the shared, common factors. From the factors of 45 and 30, the common factors are 3, 5, and 15. Thus, 15 is the greatest common factor, as it's the largest number.

The **least common multiple** is the smallest number that's a multiple of two numbers. For example, to find the least common multiple of 4 and 9, the multiples of 4 and 9 are found first. The multiples of 4 are 4, 8, 12, 16, 20, 24, 28, 32, 36, and so on. For 9, the multiples are 9, 18, 27, 36, 45, 54, etc. Thus, the least common multiple of 4 and 9 is 36, the lowest number where 4 and 9 share multiples.

If two numbers share no factors besides 1 in common, then their least common multiple will be simply their product. If two numbers have common factors, then their least common multiple will be their product divided by their greatest common factor. This can be visualized by the formula $LCM = \frac{x \times y}{GCF}$, where x and y are some integers, and LCM and GCF are their least common multiple and greatest common factor, respectively.

Operations with Fractions

A **fraction** is an equation that represents a part of a whole but can also be used to present ratios or division problems. An example of a fraction is $\frac{x}{y}$. In this example, x is called the **numerator**, while y is the

49

denominator. The numerator represents the number of parts, and the denominator is the total number of parts. They are separated by a line or slash, known as a fraction bar. In simple fractions, the numerator and denominator can be nearly any integer. However, the denominator of a fraction can never be zero because dividing by zero is a function which is undefined.

Fractions come in three different varieties: proper fractions, improper fractions, and mixed numbers. **Proper fractions** have a numerator less than the denominator, such as $\frac{3}{8}$, but **improper fractions** have a numerator greater than the denominator, such as:

$$\frac{7}{2}$$

Mixed numbers combine a whole number with a proper fraction, such as:

$$3\frac{1}{2}$$

Any mixed number can be written as an improper fraction by multiplying the integer by the denominator, adding the product to the value of the numerator, and dividing the sum by the original denominator. For example:

$$3\frac{1}{2}$$

$$\frac{3 \times 2 + 1}{2}$$

$$\frac{7}{2}$$

Whole numbers can also be converted into fractions by placing the whole number as the numerator and making the denominator 1. For example:

$$3 = \frac{3}{1}$$

One of the most fundamental concepts of fractions is their ability to be manipulated by multiplication or division. This is possible since $\frac{n}{n}$ = 1 for any non-zero integer. As a result, multiplying or dividing by $\frac{n}{n}$ will not alter the original fraction since any number multiplied or divided by 1 doesn't change the value of that number. Fractions of the same value are known as equivalent fractions. For example, $\frac{2}{4}, \frac{4}{8}, \frac{50}{100}$, and $\frac{75}{150}$ are equivalent, as they all equal $\frac{1}{2}$.

Of the four basic operations that can be performed on fractions, the one that involves the least amount of work is multiplication. To multiply two fractions, the numerators are multiplied, the denominators are multiplied, and the products are placed together as a fraction. Whole numbers and mixed numbers can also be expressed as a fraction which more easily facilitates multiplication with another fraction.

The following problems provide examples:

$$1. \frac{2}{5} \times \frac{3}{4} = \frac{6}{20} = \frac{3}{10}$$

$$2. \frac{4}{9} \times \frac{7}{11} = \frac{28}{99}$$

Dividing fractions is similar to multiplication with one key difference. To divide fractions, the numerator and denominator of the second fraction are flipped, and then one proceeds as if it were a multiplication problem:

$$1. \frac{7}{8} \div \frac{4}{5} = \frac{7}{8} \times \frac{5}{4} = \frac{35}{32}$$

$$2. \frac{5}{9} \div \frac{1}{3} = \frac{5}{9} \times \frac{3}{1} = \frac{15}{9} = \frac{5}{3}$$

Addition and subtraction require more steps than multiplication and division, as these operations require the fractions to have the same denominator, also called a **common denominator**. It is always possible to find a common denominator by multiplying the denominators. However, when the denominators are large numbers, this method is unwieldy, especially if the answer must be provided in its simplest form. Thus, it's beneficial to find the least common denominator of the fractions—the least common denominator is incidentally also the least common multiple.

Once equivalent fractions have been found with common denominators, the numerators are simply added or subtracted to arrive at the answer:

$$1. \frac{1}{2} + \frac{3}{4} = \frac{2}{4} + \frac{3}{4} = \frac{5}{4}$$

$$2. \frac{3}{12} + \frac{11}{20} = \frac{15}{60} + \frac{33}{60} = \frac{48}{60} = \frac{4}{5}$$

$$3. \frac{7}{9} - \frac{4}{15} = \frac{35}{45} - \frac{12}{45} = \frac{23}{45}$$

$$4. \frac{5}{6} - \frac{7}{18} = \frac{15}{18} - \frac{7}{18} = \frac{8}{18} = \frac{4}{9}$$

Percentages

Percentages can be thought of as fractions with a denominator of 100. In fact, percentage means "per hundred." Problems often require converting numbers from percentages, fractions, and decimals. The following explains how to work through those conversions.

Converting Fractions to Percentages

The fraction is converted by using an equivalent fraction with a denominator of 100. For example:

$$\frac{3}{4}$$

$$\frac{3}{4} \times \frac{25}{25}$$

$$\frac{75}{100}$$

$$75\%$$

51

Converting Percentages to Fractions: Percentages can be converted to fractions by turning the percentage into a fraction with a denominator of 100. Test takers should be wary of questions asking the converted fraction to be written in the simplest form. For example, $35\% = \frac{35}{100}$ which, although correctly written, has a numerator and denominator with a greatest common factor of 5, so it can be simplified to $\frac{7}{20}$.

Converting Percentages to Decimals: Because a percentage is based on "per hundred," decimals and percentages can be converted by multiplying or dividing by 100. Practically speaking, this always amounts to moving the decimal point two places to the right or left, depending on the conversion. To convert a percentage to a decimal, the decimal point is moved two places to the left and the % sign gets removed. To convert a decimal to a percentage, the decimal point is moved two places to the right and a "%" sign is added. Here are some examples:

65% = 0.65

0.33 = 33%

0.215 = 21.5%

99.99% = 0.9999

500% = 5.00

7.55 = 755%

Properties of Rational and Irrational Numbers

All real numbers can be separated into two groups: rational and irrational numbers. **Rational numbers** are any numbers that can be written as a fraction, such as $\frac{1}{3}, \frac{7}{4}$, and -25. Alternatively, **irrational numbers** are those that cannot be written as a fraction, such as numbers with never-ending, non-repeating decimal values. Many irrational numbers result from taking roots, such as $\sqrt{2}$ or $\sqrt{3}$. An irrational number may be written as:

$$34.5684952\ldots$$

The ellipsis (...) represents the line of numbers after the decimal that does not repeat and is never-ending.

When rational and irrational numbers interact, there are different types of number outcomes. For example, when adding or multiplying two rational numbers, the result is a rational number. No matter what two fractions are added or multiplied together, the result can always be written as a fraction. The following expression shows two rational numbers multiplied together:

$$\frac{3}{8} \times \frac{4}{7} = \frac{12}{56}$$

The product of these two fractions is another fraction that can be simplified to $\frac{3}{14}$.

As another interaction, rational numbers added to irrational numbers will always result in irrational numbers. No part of any fraction can be added to a never-ending, non-repeating decimal to make a rational number. The same result is true when multiplying a rational and irrational number. Taking a fractional part of a never-ending, non-repeating decimal will always result in another never-ending, non-repeating decimal. An example of the product of rational and irrational numbers is shown in the following expression: $2 \times \sqrt{7}$.

The last type of interaction concerns two irrational numbers, where the sum or product may be rational or irrational depending on the numbers being used. The following expression shows a rational sum from two irrational numbers:

$$\sqrt{3} + \left(6 - \sqrt{3}\right) = 6$$

The product of two irrational numbers can be rational or irrational. A rational result can be seen in the following expression:

$$\sqrt{2} \times \sqrt{8} = \sqrt{2 \times 8} = \sqrt{16} = 4$$

An irrational result can be seen in the following:

$$\sqrt{3} \times \sqrt{2} = \sqrt{6}$$

Rewriting Expressions Involving Radicals and Rational Exponents

Exponents are used in mathematics to express a number or variable multiplied by itself a certain number of times. For example, x^3 means x is multiplied by itself three times. In this expression, x is called the **base**, and 3 is the **exponent**. Exponents can be used in more complex problems when they contain fractions and negative numbers.

Fractional exponents can be explained by looking first at the inverse of exponents, which are **roots**. Given the expression x^2, the square root can be taken, $\sqrt{x^2}$, cancelling out the 2 and leaving x by itself, if x is positive. Cancellation occurs because $\sqrt{x}$ can be written with exponents, instead of roots, as $x^{\frac{1}{2}}$. The numerator of 1 is the exponent, and the denominator of 2 is called the root (which is why it's referred to as square root). Taking the square root of x^2 is the same as raising it to the $\frac{1}{2}$ power. Written out in mathematical form, it takes the following progression:

$$\sqrt{x^2} = (x^2)^{\frac{1}{2}} = x$$

From properties of exponents, $2 \times \frac{1}{2} = 1$ is the actual exponent of x. Another example can be seen with $x^{\frac{4}{7}}$. The variable x, raised to four-sevenths, is equal to the seventh root of x to the fourth power: $\sqrt[7]{x^4}$. In general,

$$x^{\frac{1}{n}} = \sqrt[n]{x}$$

and

$$x^{\frac{m}{n}} = \sqrt[n]{x^m}$$

53

Negative exponents also involve fractions. Whereas y^3 can also be rewritten as $\frac{y^3}{1}$, y^{-3} can be rewritten as $\frac{1}{y^3}$. A negative exponent means the exponential expression must be moved to the opposite spot in a fraction to make the exponent positive. If the negative appears in the numerator, it moves to the denominator. If the negative appears in the denominator, it is moved to the numerator. In general, $a^{-n} = \frac{1}{a^n}$, and a^{-n} and a^n are reciprocals.

Take, for example, the following expression:

$$\frac{a^{-4}b^2}{c^{-5}}$$

Since a is raised to the negative fourth power, it can be moved to the denominator. Since c is raised to the negative fifth power, it can be moved to the numerator. The b variable is raised to the positive second power, so it does not move.

The simplified expression is as follows:

$$\frac{b^2c^5}{a^4}$$

In mathematical expressions containing exponents and other operations, the order of operations must be followed. *PEMDAS* states that exponents are calculated after any parentheses and grouping symbols but before any multiplication, division, addition, and subtraction.

Scientific Notation

Scientific notation is used to represent numbers that are either very small or very large. For example, the distance to the sun is approximately 150,000,000,000 meters. Instead of writing this number with so many zeros, it can be written in scientific notation as 1.5×10^{11} meters. The same is true for very small numbers, but the exponent becomes negative. If the mass of a human cell is 0.000000000001 kilograms, that measurement can be easily represented by 1.0×10^{-12} kilograms. In both situations, scientific notation makes the measurement easier to read and understand. Each number is translated to an expression with one digit in the tens place times an expression corresponding to the zeros.

When two measurements are given and both involve scientific notation, it is important to know how these interact with each other:

- In addition and subtraction, the exponent on the ten must be the same before any operations are performed on the numbers. For example,

$$(1.3 \times 10^4) + (3.0 \times 10^3)$$

  This cannot be added until one of the exponents on the ten is changed. The 3.0×10^3 can be changed to 0.3×10^4, then the 1.3 and 0.3 can be added. The answer comes out to be 1.6×10^4.

- For multiplication, the first numbers can be multiplied and then the exponents on the tens can be added. Once an answer is formed, it may have to be converted into scientific notation again depending on the change that occurred.

54

- The following is an example of multiplication with scientific notation:

$$(4.5 \times 10^3) \times (3.0 \times 10^{-5}) = 13.5 \times 10^{-2}$$

- Since this answer is not in scientific notation, the decimal is moved over to the left one unit, and 1 is added to the ten's exponent. This results in the final answer: 1.35×10^{-1}.

- For division, the first numbers are divided, and the exponents on the tens are subtracted. Again, the answer may need to be converted into scientific notation form, depending on the type of changes that occurred during the problem.

- Order of magnitude relates to scientific notation and is the total count of powers of 10 in a number. For example, there are 6 orders of magnitude in 1,000,000. If a number is raised by an order of magnitude, it is multiplied times 10. Order of magnitude can be helpful in estimating results using very large or small numbers. An answer should make sense in terms of its order of magnitude.

- For example, if area is calculated using two dimensions with 6 orders of magnitude, because area involves multiplication, the answer should have around 12 orders of magnitude. Also, answers can be estimated by rounding to the largest place value in each number. For example, 5,493,302×2,523,100 can be estimated by $5 \times 3 = 15$ with 6 orders of magnitude.

Reasoning Quantitatively

Dimensional analysis is the process of converting between different units using equivalent measurement statements. For example, running a 5K is the same as running approximately 3.1 miles. This conversion can be found by knowing that 1 kilometer is equal to approximately 0.62 miles.

The following calculation shows how to convert kilometers into miles. The original units need to be opposite one another in each of the two fractions: one in the original amount and one in the denominator of the conversion factor. This specific example consists of 5 km being multiplied times the conversion factor .62 mi/km. By design, quantities in kilometers are opposite one another and therefore cancel, leaving 3.11 miles as the converted result.

$$5km \times \left(\frac{0.62 miles}{1km} \right) = 3.11 \ miles$$

Units are also important throughout formulas in calculating quantities such as volume and area. To find the volume of a pyramid, the following formula is used: $V = \frac{1}{3}Bh$. B is the area of the base, and h is the height. In the example shown below, two of the same type of dimension are composed of two different units. All dimensions must be converted to the same units before plugging values into the formula for volume.

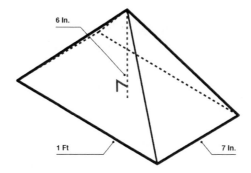

In this case, all lengths will be converted to inches. To find the area of the base, it's necessary to convert 1 ft. to 12 inches. Then, the area of the base can be calculated as:

$$B = 12 \ in \times 7 \ in = 84 \ in^2$$

B can then be substituted into the volume formula as follows:

$$V = \frac{1}{3}(84in^2)(6in) = 168 \ in^3$$

Formulas are a common situation in which units need to be interpreted and used. However, graphs can also carry meaning through units. The following graph is an example. It represents a graph of the position of an object over time. The m axis represents the number of meters the object is from the starting point at time s, in seconds. Interpreting this graph, the origin shows that at time zero seconds, the object is zero meters away from the starting point. As the time increases to one second, the position increases to five meters away. This trend continues until 6 seconds, where the object is 30 meters away from the starting position. After this point in time—since the graph remains horizontal from 6 to 10 seconds—the object must have stopped moving.

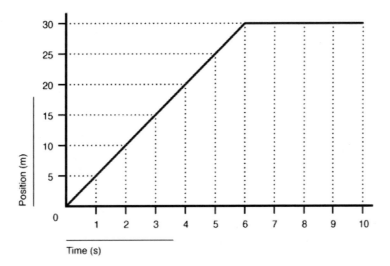

In each of the previous problem examples, the units were important to the answer. When solving problems with units, it's important to consider the reasonableness of the answer. If conversions are used, it's helpful to have an estimated value to compare the final answer to. This way, if the final answer is too distant from the estimate, it will be obvious that a mistake was made.

Choosing a Level of Accuracy

Precision and accuracy are used to describe groups of measurements. **Precision** describes a group of measures that are very close together, regardless of whether the measures are close to the true value. **Accuracy** describes how close the measures are to the true value.

The following graphic illustrates the different combinations that may occur with different groups of measures:

| Low accuracy | Low accuracy | High accuracy | High accuracy |
| Low precision | High precision | Low precision | High precision |

Since accuracy refers to the closeness of a value to the true measurement, the level of accuracy depends on the object measured and the instrument used to measure it. This will vary depending on the situation. If measuring the mass of a set of dictionaries, kilograms may be used as the units. In this case, it is not vitally important to have a high level of accuracy. If the measurement is a few grams away from the true value, the discrepancy might not make a big difference in the problem.

57

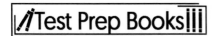

In a different situation, the level of accuracy may be more significant. Pharmacists need to be sure they are very accurate in their measurements of medicines that they give to patients. In this case, the level of accuracy is vitally important and not something to be estimated. In the dictionary situation, the measurements were given as whole numbers in kilograms. In the pharmacist's situation, the measurements for medicine must be taken to the milligram and sometimes further, depending on the type of medicine.

When considering the accuracy of measurements, the error in each measurement can be shown as absolute and relative. **Absolute error** tells the actual difference between the measured value and the true value. The **relative error** tells how large the error is in relation to the true value. There may be two problems where the absolute error of the measurements is 10 grams. For one problem, this may mean the relative error is very small because the measured value is 14,990 grams, and the true value is 15,000 grams. Ten grams in relation to the true value of 15,000 is small: 0.06%. For the other problem, the measured value is 290 grams, and the true value is 300 grams. In this case, the 10-gram absolute error means a high relative error because the true value is smaller. The relative error is 10/300 = 0.03, or 3%.

Solving Multistep Real-World Problems

Ratios are used to show the relationship between two quantities. The ratio of oranges to apples in the grocery store may be 3 to 2. That means that for every 3 oranges, there are 2 apples. This comparison can be expanded to represent the actual number of oranges and apples, such as 36 oranges to 24 apples. Another example may be the number of boys to girls in a math class. If the ratio of boys to girls is given as 2 to 5, that means there are 2 boys to every 5 girls in the class. Ratios can also be compared if the units in each ratio are the same. The ratio of boys to girls in the math class can be compared to the ratio of boys to girls in a science class by stating which ratio is higher and which is lower.

Rates are used to compare two quantities with different units. **Unit rates** are the simplest form of rate. With unit rates, the denominator in the comparison of two units is one. For example, if someone can type at a rate of 1,000 words in 5 minutes, then their unit rate for typing is $\frac{1,000}{5} = 200$ words in one minute or 200 words per minute. Any rate can be converted into a unit rate by dividing to make the denominator one. 1,000 words in 5 minutes has been converted into the unit rate of 200 words per minute.

The ratio between two similar geometric figures is called the **scale factor**. In the following example, there are two similar triangles. The scale factor from figure A to figure B is 2 because the length of the corresponding side of the larger triangle, 14, is twice the corresponding side on the smaller triangle, 7.

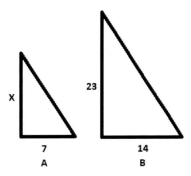

This scale factor can also be used to find the value of X. Since the scale factor from small to large is 2, the larger number, 23, can be divided by 2 to find the missing side: $X = 11.5$. The scale factor can also be represented in the equation $2A = B$ because two times the lengths of A gives the corresponding lengths of B. This is the idea behind similar triangles.

Much like a scale factor can be written using an equation like $2A = B$, a **proportional relationship** is represented by the equation $Y = kX$. X and Y are proportional because as values in X increase, the values in Y also increase. A relationship that is inversely proportional can be represented by the equation $Y = \frac{k}{X}$, where the value of Y decreases as the value of X increases and vice versa. The following graph represents these two types of relationships between x and y. The grey line represents a proportional relationship because the y-values increase as the x-values increase.

The black line represents an inversely-proportional relationship because the y-values decrease as the x-values increase.

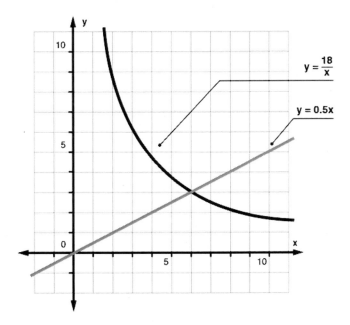

Proportional reasoning can be used to solve problems involving ratios, percentages, and averages. Ratios can be used in setting up proportions and solving them to find unknowns. For example, if someone averages 10 pages of math homework completed in 3 nights, how long would it take him or her to complete 22 pages? Both ratios can be written as fractions. The second ratio would contain the unknown. The following proportion represents this problem where x is the unknown number of nights:

$$\frac{10\ pages}{3\ nights} = \frac{22\ pages}{x\ nights}$$

Solving this proportion entails cross-multiplying and results in the following equation:

$$10x = 22 \times 3$$

Simplifying and solving for x results in the exact solution: $x = 6.6\ nights$. The result would be rounded up to 7 because the homework would actually be completed on the 7th night.

The following problem uses ratios involving percentages:

If 20% of the class is girls and 30 students are in the class, how many girls are in the class?

To set up this problem, it is helpful to use the common proportion:

$$\frac{\%}{100} = \frac{is}{of}$$

Within the proportion, % is the percentage of girls, 100 is the total percentage of the class, *is* is the number of girls, and *of* is the total number of students in the class. Most percentage problems can be written using this language. To solve this problem, the proportion should be set up as $\frac{20}{100} = \frac{x}{30}$, then solved for x. Cross-multiplying results in the equation,

$$20 \times 30 = 100x$$

This results in the solution $x = 6$. There are 6 girls in the class.

Ratios can be used to solve problems that concern length, volume, and other units. If the following graphic of a cone is given, the problem may ask for the volume to be found.

Referring to the formulas provided on the test, the volume of a cone is given as: $V = \pi r^2 \frac{h}{3}$, where r is the radius, and h is the height. Plugging $r = 8$ and $h = 15$ from the graphic into the formula, the following is obtained:

$$V = \pi(8^2)\frac{15}{3}$$

Therefore, the volume of the cone is found to be 1005.3m³. Sometimes, answers in different units are sought. If this problem wanted the answer in liters, 1005.3m³ would need to be converted. Using the equivalence statement 1m³ = 1,000L, the following ratio would be used to solve for liters:

$$1,005.3\text{m}^3 \times \frac{1,000L}{1m^3}$$

Cubic meters in the numerator and denominator cancel each other out, and the answer is converted to 1,005,300 liters, or 1.0053×10^6 L.

Algebra

Interpreting Parts of an Expression

Algebraic expressions are built out of monomials. A **monomial** is a variable raised to some power multiplied by a constant: ax^n, where a is any constant and n is a whole number. A constant is also a monomial.

A **polynomial** is a sum of monomials. Examples of polynomials include:

$$3x^4 + 2x^2 - x - 3$$

$$\frac{4}{5}x^3$$

The latter is also a monomial. If the highest power of x is 1, the polynomial is called **linear**. If the highest power of x is 2, it is called **quadratic**.

Algebraic Functions

A function is called **algebraic** if it is built up from polynomials by adding, subtracting, multiplying, dividing, and taking radicals. This means that, for example, the variable can never appear in an exponent. Thus, polynomials and rational functions are algebraic, but exponential functions are not algebraic. It turns out that logarithms and trigonometric functions are not algebraic either.

A function of the form:

$$f(x) = a_n x^n + a_{n-1}x^{n-1} + a_{n-2}x^{n-2} + \ldots + a_1 x + a_0$$

is called a polynomial function. The value of n is called the degree of the polynomial. In the case where $n = 1$, it is called a linear function. In the case where $n = 2$, it is called a quadratic function. In the case where $n = 3$, it is called a cubic function.

When n is even, the polynomial is called even, and not all real numbers will be in its range. When n is odd, the polynomial is called odd, and the range includes all real numbers.

The graph of a quadratic function below will be a parabola:

$$f(x) = ax^2 + bx + c$$

61

To see whether or not the parabola opens up or down, it's necessary to check the coefficient of x^2, which is the value a.

If the coefficient is positive, then the parabola opens upward. If the coefficient is negative, then the parabola opens downward.

Exponential Functions

An **exponential function** is a function of the form $f(x) = b^x$, where b is a positive real number other than 1. In such a function, b is called the **base**.

The **domain** of an exponential function is all real numbers, and the **range** is all positive real numbers. There will always be a horizontal asymptote of $y = 0$ on one side. If b is greater than 1, then the graph will be increasing moving to the right. If b is less than 1, then the graph will be decreasing moving to the right. Exponential functions are one-to-one. The basic exponential function graph will go through the point $(0,1)$.

<u>Example</u>
Solve $5^{x+1} = 25$.

Get the x out of the exponent by rewriting the equation $5^{x+1} = 5^2$ so that both sides have a base of 5.

Since the bases are the same, the exponents must be equal to each other.

This leaves $x + 1 = 2$ or $x = 1$.

To check the answer, the x-value of 1 can be substituted back into the original equation.

Performing Arithmetic Operations on Polynomials and Rational Expressions

Addition and subtraction operations can be performed on polynomials with like terms. **Like terms** refers to terms that have the same variable and exponent. The two following polynomials can be added together by collecting like terms:

$$(x^2 + 3x - 4) + (4x^2 - 7x + 8)$$

The x^2 terms can be added as:

$$x^2 + 4x^2 = 5x^2$$

The x terms can be added as $3x + -7x = -4x$, and the constants can be added as:

$$-4 + 8 = 4$$

The following expression is the result of the addition:

$$5x^2 - 4x + 4$$

When subtracting polynomials, the same steps are followed, only subtracting like terms together.

Multiplication of polynomials can also be performed. Given the two polynomials, $(y^3 - 4)$ and $(x^2 + 8x - 7)$, each term in the first polynomial must be multiplied by each term in the second polynomial. The steps to multiply each term in the given example are as follows:

$$(y^3 \times x^2) + (y^3 \times 8x) + (y^3 \times -7) + (-4 \times x^2) + (-4 \times 8x) + (-4 \times -7)$$

Simplifying each multiplied part, yields:

$$x^2y^3 + 8xy^3 - 7y^3 - 4x^2 - 32x + 28$$

None of the terms can be combined because there are no like terms in the final expression. Any polynomials can be multiplied by each other by following the same set of steps, then collecting like terms at the end.

Polynomial Identities

Difference of squares refers to a binomial composed of the difference of two squares. For example, $a^2 - b^2$ is a difference of squares. It can be written $(a)^2 - (b)^2$, and it can be factored into $(a - b)(a + b)$. Recognizing the difference of squares allows the expression to be rewritten easily because of the form it takes. For some expressions, factoring consists of more than one step. When factoring, it's important to always check to make sure that the result cannot be factored further. If it can, then the expression should be split further. If it cannot be, the factoring step is complete, and the expression is completely factored.

A sum and difference of cubes is another way to factor a polynomial expression. When the polynomial takes the form of addition or subtraction of two terms that can be written as a cube, a formula is given. The following graphic shows the factorization of a difference of cubes:

$$a^3 - b^3 = (a - b)(a^2 + ab + b^2)$$

same sign

opposite sign

always +

This form of factoring can be useful in finding the zeros of a function of degree 3. For example, when solving $x^3 - 27 = 0$, this rule needs to be used. $x^3 - 27$ is first written as the difference two cubes, $(x)^3 - (3)^3$ and then factored into:

$$(x - 3)(x^2 + 3x + 9)$$

This expression may not be factored any further. Each factor is then set equal to zero. Therefore, one solution is found to be $x = 3$, and the other two solutions must be found using the quadratic formula. A sum of squares would have a similar process. The formula for factoring a sum of cubes is:

$$a^3 + b^3 = (a + b)(a^2 - ab + b^2)$$

Math

The opposite of factoring is multiplying. Multiplying a square of a binomial involves the following rules:

$$(a + b)^2 = a^2 + 2ab + b^2$$

$$(a - b)^2 = a^2 - 2ab + b^2$$

Rational Expressions

A fraction, or ratio, wherein each part is a polynomial, defines **rational expressions**. Some examples include:

$$\frac{2x + 6}{x}$$

$$\frac{1}{x^2 - 4x + 8}$$

$$\frac{z^2}{x + 5}$$

Exponents on the variables are restricted to whole numbers, which means roots and negative exponents are not included in rational expressions.

Rational expressions can be transformed by factoring. For example, the expression $\frac{x^2-5x+6}{(x-3)}$ can be rewritten by factoring the numerator to obtain:

$$\frac{(x - 3)(x - 2)}{(x - 3)}$$

Therefore, the common binomial $(x - 3)$ can cancel so that the simplified expression is:

$$\frac{(x - 2)}{1} = (x - 2)$$

Additionally, other rational expressions can be rewritten to take on different forms. Some may be factorable in themselves, while others can be transformed through arithmetic operations. Rational expressions are closed under addition, subtraction, multiplication, and division by a nonzero expression. **Closed** means that if any one of these operations is performed on a rational expression, the result will still be a rational expression. The set of all real numbers is another example of a set closed under all four operations.

Adding and subtracting rational expressions is based on the same concepts as adding and subtracting simple fractions. For both concepts, the denominators must be the same for the operation to take place.

For example, here are two rational expressions:

$$\frac{x^3 - 4}{(x - 3)} + \frac{x + 8}{(x - 3)}$$

Since the denominators are both $(x - 3)$, the numerators can be combined by collecting like terms to form:

64

$$\frac{x^3 + x + 4}{(x - 3)}$$

If the denominators are different, they need to be made common (the same) by using the **Least Common Denominator (LCD)**. Each denominator needs to be factored, and the LCD contains each factor that appears in any one denominator the greatest number of times it appears in any denominator. The original expressions need to be multiplied times a form of 1, which will turn each denominator into the LCD. This process is like adding fractions with unlike denominators. It is also important when working with rational expressions to define what value of the variable makes the denominator zero. For this particular value, the expression is undefined.

Multiplication of rational expressions is performed like multiplication of fractions. The numerators are multiplied; then, the denominators are multiplied. The final fraction is then simplified. The expressions are simplified by factoring and cancelling out common terms. In the following example, the numerator of the second expression can be factored first to simplify the expression before multiplying:

$$\frac{x^2}{(x - 4)} \times \frac{x^2 - x - 12}{2}$$

$$\frac{x^2}{(x - 4)} \times \frac{(x - 4)(x + 3)}{2}$$

The $(x - 4)$ on the top and bottom cancel out:

$$\frac{x^2}{1} \times \frac{(x + 3)}{2}$$

Then multiplication is performed, resulting in:

$$\frac{x^3 + 3x^2}{2}$$

Dividing rational expressions is similar to the division of fractions, where division turns into multiplying by a reciprocal. The following expression can be rewritten as a multiplication problem:

$$\frac{x^2 - 3x + 7}{x - 4} \div \frac{x^2 - 5x + 3}{x - 4}$$

$$\frac{x^2 - 3x + 7}{x - 4} \times \frac{x - 4}{x^2 - 5x + 3}$$

The $x - 4$ cancels out, leaving:

$$\frac{x^2 - 3x + 7}{x^2 - 5x + 3}$$

The final answers should always be completely simplified. If a function is composed of a rational expression, the zeros of the graph can be found from setting the polynomial in the numerator as equal to zero and solving. The values that make the denominator equal to zero will either exist on the graph as a hole or a vertical asymptote.

Writing Expressions in Equivalent Forms

Algebraic expressions are made up of numbers, variables, and combinations of the two, using mathematical operations. Expressions can be rewritten based on their factors. For example, the expression $6x + 4$ can be rewritten as $2(3x + 2)$ because 2 is a factor of both $6x$ and 4. More complex expressions can also be rewritten based on their factors. The expression $x^4 - 16$ can be rewritten as,

$$(x^2 - 4)(x^2 + 4)$$

This is a different type of factoring, where a difference of squares is factored into a sum and difference of the same two terms. With some expressions, the factoring process is simple and only leads to a different way to represent the expression. With others, factoring and rewriting the expression leads to more information about the given problem.

In the following quadratic equation, factoring the binomial leads to finding the zeros of the function:

$$x^2 - 5x + 6 = y$$

This equation factors into:

$$(x - 3)(x - 2) = y$$

2 and 3 are found to be the zeros of the function when y is set equal to zero. The zeros of any function are the x-values where the graph of the function on the coordinate plane crosses the x-axis.

Exponential expressions can also be rewritten, just as quadratic equations. Properties of exponents must be understood. Multiplying two exponential expressions with the same base involves adding the exponents:

$$a^m a^n = a^{m+n}$$

Dividing two exponential expressions with the same base involves subtracting the exponents:

$$\frac{a^m}{a^n} = a^{m-n}$$

Raising an exponential expression to another exponent includes multiplying the exponents:

$$(a^m)^n = a^{mn}$$

The zero power always gives a value of 1:

$$a^0 = 1$$

Raising either a product or a fraction to a power involves distributing that power:

$$(ab)^m = a^m b^m \text{ and } \left(\frac{a}{b}\right)^m = \frac{a^m}{b^m}$$

Finally, raising a number to a negative exponent is equivalent to the reciprocal including the positive exponent:

$$a^{-m} = \frac{1}{a^m}$$

66

Finding the Zeros of a Function

The zeros of a function are the points where its graph crosses the x-axis. At these points, $y = 0$. One way to find the zeros is to analyze the graph. If given the graph, the x-coordinates can be found where the line crosses the x-axis. Another way to find the zeros is to set $y = 0$ in the equation and solve for x. Depending on the type of equation, this could be done by using opposite operations, by factoring the equation, by completing the square, or by using the quadratic formula. If a graph does not cross the x-axis, then the function may have complex roots.

Solving Linear Equations and Inequalities

The sum of a number and 5 is equal to -8 times the number. To find this unknown number, a simple equation can be written to represent the problem. Key words such as difference, equal, and times are used to form the following equation with one variable:

$$n + 5 = -8n$$

When solving for n, opposite operations are used. First, n is subtracted from $-8n$ across the equals sign, resulting in $5 = -9n$. Then, -9 is divided on both sides, leaving $n = -\frac{5}{9}$. This solution can be graphed on the number line with a dot as shown below:

If the problem were changed to say, "The sum of a number and 5 is greater than -8 times the number," then an inequality would be used instead of an equation. Using key words again, *greater than* is represented by the symbol >. The inequality $n + 5 > -8n$ can be solved using the same techniques, resulting in $n < -\frac{5}{9}$. The only time solving an inequality differs from solving an equation is when a negative number is either multiplied times or divided by each side of the inequality. The sign must be switched in this case. For this example, the graph of the solution changes to the following graph because the solution represents all real numbers less than $-\frac{5}{9}$. Not included in this solution is $-\frac{5}{9}$ because it is a *less than* symbol, not *equal to*.

Equations and inequalities in two variables represent a relationship. Jim owns a car wash and charges $40 per car. The rent for the facility is $350 per month. An equation can be written to relate the number of cars Jim cleans to the money he makes per month. Let x represent the number of cars and y represent the profit Jim makes each month from the car wash. The equation $y = 40x - 350$ can be used to show Jim's profit or loss. Since this equation has two variables, the coordinate plane can be used to show the relationship and predict profit or loss for Jim. The following graph shows that Jim must wash at least nine cars to pay the rent, where $x = 9$. Anything nine cars and above yield a profit shown in the value on the y-axis.

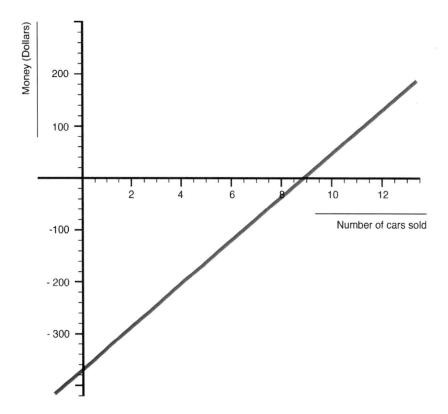

With a single equation in two variables, the solutions are limited only by the situation the equation represents. When two equations or inequalities are used, more constraints are added. For example, in a system of linear equations, there is often—although not always—only one answer. The point of intersection of two lines is the solution. For a system of inequalities, there are infinitely many answers. The intersection of two solution sets gives the solution set of the system of inequalities.

Given a linear inequality, if the inequality symbol is replaced by an equals sign, this line can be graphed. Then, if the original symbol was < or >, either one side or the other represents all ordered pairs that satisfy this inequality. If the original symbol was ≤ or ≥, then either one side or the other plus the line represents all ordered pairs that satisfy this inequality.

Therefore, in order to graph a linear inequality, the line must be plotted first. If < or > is used, a dashed line is used to represent the line. If ≤ or ≥ is used, then a solid line is used to represent the line. Once the line is graphed, a test point is chosen on either side of the line. If, when plugged into the original inequality, the process results in a true statement, that side of the line is shaded in. If, when plugged into the original inequality, the process results in a false statement, the other side of the line is shaded in. Here is an example of a graph of a linear inequality:

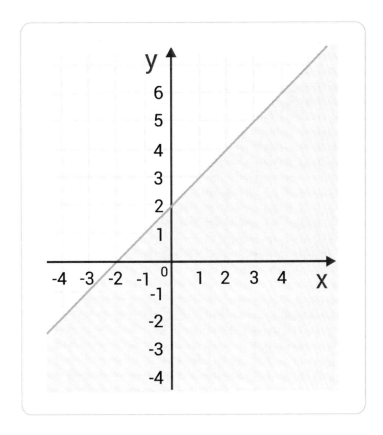

Formulas with two variables are equations used to represent a specific relationship. For example, the formula $d = rt$ represents the relationship between distance, rate, and time. If Bob travels at a rate of 35 miles per hour on his road trip from Westminster to Seneca, the formula $d = 35t$ can be used to represent his distance traveled in a specific length of time. Formulas can also be used to show different roles of the variables, transformed without any given numbers. Solving for r, the formula becomes $\frac{d}{t} = r$. The t is moved over by division so that *rate* is a function of distance and time.

Solving Equations

The letters in an equation are variables as they stand for unknown quantities that you are trying to solve for. The numbers attached to the variables by multiplication are called coefficients. *X* is commonly used as a variable, though any letter can be used. For example, in $3x - 7 = 20$, the variable is $3x$, and it needs to be isolated. The numbers (also called constants) are -7 and 20. That means $3x$ needs to be on one side of the equals sign (either side is fine), and all the numbers need to be on the other side of the equals sign.

To accomplish this, the equation must be manipulated by performing opposite operations of what already exists. Remember that addition and subtraction are opposites and that multiplication and division are opposites. Any action taken to one side of the equation must be taken on the other side to maintain equality.

69

Therefore, since the 7 is being subtracted, it can be moved to the right side of the equation by adding seven to both sides:

$$3x - 7 = 20$$

$$3x - 7 + 7 = 20 + 7$$

$$3x = 27$$

Now that the variable $3x$ is on one side and the constants (now combined into one constant) are on the other side, the 3 needs to be moved to the right side. 3 and x are being multiplied together, so 3 needs to be divided from each side.

$$\frac{3x}{3} = \frac{27}{3}$$

$$x = 9$$

Now that x has been completely isolated, we know its value.

The solution is found to be $x = 9$. This solution can be checked for accuracy by plugging $x = 9$ in the original equation. After simplifying the equation, $20 = 20$ is found, which is a true statement:

$$3 \times 9 - 7 = 20$$

$$27 - 7 = 20$$

$$20 = 20$$

Equations that require solving for a variable (algebraic equations) come in many forms. Here are some more examples:

No coefficient attached to the variable:

$$x + 8 = 20$$

$$x + 8 - 8 = 20 - 8$$

$$x = 12$$

A fractional coefficient:

$$\frac{1}{2}z + 24 = 36$$

$$\frac{1}{2}z + 24 - 24 = 36 - 24$$

$$\frac{1}{2}z = 12$$

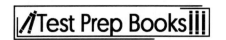

Now we multiply the fraction by its inverse:

$$\frac{2}{1} \times \frac{1}{2}z = 12 \times \frac{2}{1}$$

$$z = 24$$

Multiple examples of x:

$$14x + x - 4 = 3x + 2$$

All examples of x can be combined.

$$15x - 4 = 3x + 2$$

$$15x - 4 + 4 = 3x + 2 + 4$$

$$15x = 3x + 6$$

$$15x - 3x = 3x + 6 - 3x$$

$$12x = 6$$

$$\frac{12x}{12} = \frac{6}{12}$$

$$x = \frac{1}{2}$$

Methods for Solving Equations

Equations with one variable can be solved using the addition principle and multiplication principle. If $a = b$, then $a + c = b + c$, and $ac = bc$. Given the equation,

$$2x - 3 = 5x + 7$$

The first step is to combine the variable terms and the constant terms. Using the principles, expressions can be added and subtracted onto and off both sides of the equals sign, so the equation turns into $-10 = 3x$. Dividing by 3 on both sides through the multiplication principle with $c = \frac{1}{3}$ results in the final answer of $x = \frac{-10}{3}$.

Solving quadratic equations is a little trickier. If they take the form $ax^2 - b = 0$, then the equation can be solved by adding b to both sides and dividing by a to get:

$$x^2 = \frac{b}{a}$$

The solution is $x = \pm\sqrt{\frac{b}{a}}$. Note that this is actually two separate solutions, unless b happens to be zero.

If a quadratic equation has no constant—so that it takes the form $ax^2 + bx = 0$—then the x can be factored out to get:

$$x(ax + b) = 0$$

Then, the solutions are $x = 0$, together with the solutions to $ax + b = 0$. Both factors x and $(ax + b)$ can be set equal to zero to solve for x because one of those values must be zero for their product to equal zero. For an equation $ab = 0$ to be true, either $a = 0$, or $b = 0$.

A given quadratic equation $x^2 + bx + c$ can be factored into:

$$(x + A)(x + B)$$

$A + B = b$, and $AB = c$. Finding the values of A and B can take time, but such a pair of numbers can be found by guessing and checking. Looking at the positive and negative factors for c offers a good starting point.

For example, in $x^2 - 5x + 6$, the factors of 6 are 1, 2, and 3. Now, $(-2)(-3) = 6$, and $-2 - 3 = -5$. In general, however, this may not work, in which case another approach may need to be used.

A quadratic equation of the form $x^2 + 2xb + b^2 = 0$ can be factored into:

$$(x + b)^2 = 0$$

Similarly, $x^2 - 2xy + y^2 = 0$ factors into:

$$(x - y)^2 = 0$$

In general, the constant term may not be the right value to be factored this way. A more general method for solving these quadratic equations must then be found. The following two methods will work in any situation.

Completing the Square

Completing the square is one way to find zeros when factoring is not an option. The following equation cannot be factored:

$$x^2 + 10x - 9 = 0$$

The first step in this method is to move the constant to the right side of the equation, making it:

$$x^2 + 10x = 9$$

Then, the coefficient of x is divided by 2 and squared. This number is then added to both sides of the equation, to make the equation still true. For this example, $\left(\frac{10}{2}\right)^2 = 25$ is added to both sides of the equation to obtain:

$$x^2 + 10x + 25 = 9 + 25$$

This expression simplifies to $x^2 + 10x + 25 = 34$, which can then be factored into:

$$(x + 5)^2 = 34$$

Solving for x then involves taking the square root of both sides and subtracting 5. This leads to two zeros of the function:

$$x = \pm\sqrt{34} - 5$$

72

Depending on the type of answer the question seeks, a calculator may be used to find exact numbers.

The Quadratic Formula

The quadratic formula can be used to solve any quadratic equation. This formula may be the longest method for solving quadratic equations and is commonly used as a last resort after other methods are ruled out.

The quadratic formula is presented below:

$$x = \frac{-b \pm \sqrt{b^2 - 4ac}}{2a}$$

$a, b,$ and c are the coefficients in the original equation in standard form:

$$y = ax^2 + bx + c$$

For this equation,

$$y = x^2 - 4x + 3$$

$$x = \frac{4 \pm \sqrt{(-4)^2 - 4(1)(3)}}{2(1)}$$

$$\frac{4 \pm \sqrt{16 - 12}}{2}$$

$$\frac{4 \pm 2}{2}$$

$$1, 3$$

The expression underneath the radical is called the **discriminant**. Without working out the entire formula, the value of the discriminant can reveal the nature of the solutions. If the value of the discriminant $b^2 - 4ac$ is positive, then there will be two real solutions. If the value is zero, there will be one real solution. If the value is negative, the two solutions will be imaginary or complex. If the solutions are complex, it means that the parabola never touches the x-axis. An example of a complex solution can be found by solving the following quadratic:

$$y = x^2 - 4x + 8$$

By using the quadratic formula, the solutions are found to be:

$$x = \frac{4 \pm \sqrt{(-4)^2 - 4(1)(8)}}{2(1)}$$

$$\frac{4 \pm \sqrt{16 - 32}}{2}$$

$$\frac{4 \pm \sqrt{-16}}{2}$$

$$2 \pm 2i$$

73

The solutions both have a real part, 2, and an imaginary part, $2i$.

Solving Systems of Equations

A **system of equations** is a group of equations that have the same variables or unknowns. These equations can be linear, but they are not always so. Finding a solution to a system of equations means finding the values of the variables that satisfy each equation. For a linear system of two equations and two variables, there could be a single solution, no solution, or infinitely many solutions.

A single solution occurs when there is one value for x and y that satisfies the system. This is shown on the graph where the lines cross at exactly one point. When there is no solution, the lines are parallel and do not ever cross. With infinitely many solutions, the equations may look different, but they are the same line. One equation will be a multiple of the other, and on the graph, they lie on top of each other.

These three types of systems of linear equations are shown below:

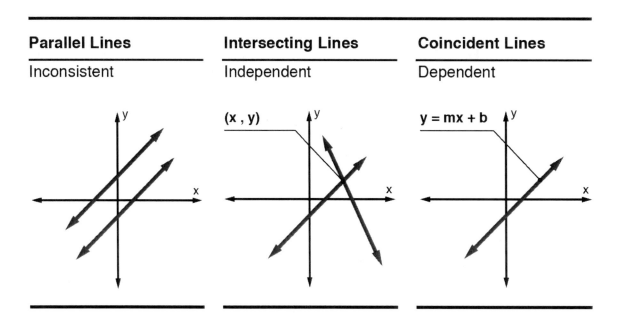

The process of elimination can be used to solve a system of equations. For example, the following equations make up a system:

$$x + 3y = 10 \text{ and } 2x - 5y = 9$$

Immediately adding these equations does not eliminate a variable, but it is possible to change the first equation by multiplying the whole equation by -2. This changes the first equation to:

$$-2x - 6y = -20$$

The equations can be then added to obtain $-11y = -11$. Solving for y yields $y = 1$. To find the rest of the solution, 1 can be substituted in for y in either original equation to find the value of $x = 7$. The solution to the system is (7, 1) because it makes both equations true, and it is the point in which the lines intersect. If the system is **dependent**—having infinitely many solutions—then both variables will

74

cancel out when the elimination method is used, resulting in an equation that is true for many values of x and y. Since the system is dependent, both equations can be simplified to the same equation, or line.

A system can also be solved using **substitution**. This involves solving one equation for a variable and then plugging that solved equation into the other equation in the system. For example, $x - y = -2$ and $3x + 2y = 9$ can be solved using substitution. The first equation can be solved for x, where:

$$x = -2 + y$$

Then it can be plugged into the other equation,

$$3(-2 + y) + 2y = 9$$

Solving for y yields $-6 + 3y + 2y = 9$, where $y = 3$. If $y = 3$, then $x = 1$. This solution can be checked by plugging in these values for the variables in each equation to see if it makes a true statement.

Finally, a solution to a system of equations can be found graphically. The solution to a linear system is the point or points where the lines cross. The values of x and y represent the coordinates (x, y) where the lines intersect. Using the same system of equations as above, they can be solved for y to put them in slope-intercept form,

$$y = mx + b$$

These equations become $y = x + 2$ and,

$$y = -\frac{3}{2}x + 4.5$$

The slope is the coefficient of x, and the y-intercept is the constant value. This system with the solution is shown below:

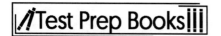

A system of equations may also be made up of a linear and a quadratic equation. These systems may have one solution, two solutions, or no solutions. The graph of these systems involves one straight line and one parabola. Algebraically, these systems can be solved by solving the linear equation for one variable and plugging that answer in to the quadratic equation. If possible, the equation can then be solved to find part of the answer. The graphing method is commonly used for these types of systems. On a graph, these two lines can be found to intersect at one point, at two points across the parabola, or at no points.

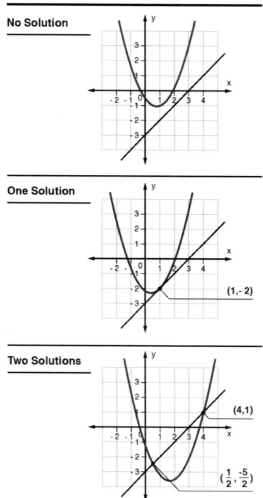

Representing and Solving Equations and Inequalities Graphically

Systems of linear inequalities are like systems of equations, but the solutions are different. Since inequalities have infinitely many solutions, their systems also have infinitely many solutions. Finding the solutions of inequalities involves graphs. A system of two equations and two inequalities is linear; thus, the lines can be graphed using slope-intercept form. If the inequality has an equals sign, the line is solid. If the inequality only has a greater than or less than symbol, the line on the graph is dotted. Dashed lines

76

indicate that points lying on the line are not included in the solution. After the lines are graphed, a region is shaded on one side of the line. This side is found by determining if a point—known as a *test point*—lying on one side of the line produces a true inequality. If it does, that side of the graph is shaded. If the point produces a false inequality, the line is shaded on the opposite side from the point. The graph of a system of inequalities involves shading the intersection of the two shaded regions. An example of a system of linear inequalities is shown below. The smaller shaded region that overlaps both larger shaded regions is the solution to the system. Any point that lies in this region or on the solid line in that region produces a true inequality for either inequality used.

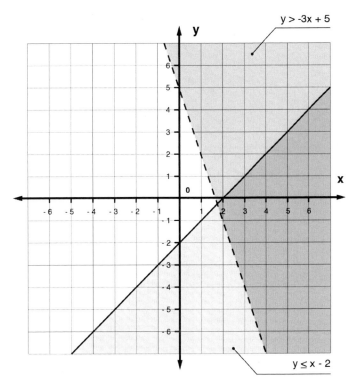

An ordered pair (x, y) on either side of the line should be chosen to test in the inequality statement. If substituting the values for x and y results in a true statement ($15(3) + 25(2) > 90$), that ordered pair and all others on that side of the boundary line are part of the solution set. To indicate this, that region of the graph should be shaded. If substituting the ordered pair results in a false statement, the ordered pair and all others on that side are not part of the solution set. Therefore, the other region of the graph contains the solutions and should be shaded.

A question may simply ask whether a given ordered pair is a solution to a given inequality. To determine this, the values should be substituted for the ordered pair into the inequality. If the result is a true statement, the ordered pair is a solution; if the result is a false statement, the ordered pair is not a solution.

Creating Equations and Inequalities to Represent Relationships

An algebraic expression is a statement about unknown quantities expressed in mathematical symbols. The statement *five times a number added to forty* is expressed as $5x + 40$. An equation is a statement in which two expressions (with at least one containing a variable) are equal to one another. The statement *five times a number added to forty is equal to ten* is expressed as:

$$5x + 40 = 10$$

Real world scenarios can also be expressed mathematically. Suppose a job pays its employees $300 per week and $40 for each sale made. The weekly pay is represented by the expression $40x + 300$ where x is the number of sales made during the week.

Consider the following scenario: Bob had $20 and Tom had $4. After selling 4 ice cream cones to Bob, Tom has as much money as Bob. The cost of an ice cream cone is an unknown quantity and can be represented by a variable (x). The amount of money Bob has after his purchase is four times the cost of an ice cream cone subtracted from his original $20 → $20 - 4x$. The amount of money Tom has after his sale is four times the cost of an ice cream cone added to his original $4 → $4x + 4$. After the sale, the amount of money that Bob and Tom have is equal:

$$20 - 4x = 4x + 4$$

Solving either equation for x will yield $4 as the price for an ice cream cone:

$$4x + 4 = 20$$

$$4x = 16$$

$$x = \$4$$

When expressing a verbal or written statement mathematically, it is vital to understand words or phrases that can be represented with symbols. The following are examples:

Symbol	Phrase
+	Added to; increased by; sum of; more than
−	Decreased by; difference between; less than; take away
×	Multiplied by; 3(4, 5...) times as large; product of
÷	Divided by; quotient of; half (third, etc.) of
=	Is; the same as; results in; as much as; equal to
x,t,n, etc.	A number; unknown quantity; value of; variable

Use of Formulas

Formulas are mathematical expressions that define the value of one quantity, given the value of one or more different quantities. Formulas look like equations because they contain variables, numbers, operators, and an equal sign. All formulas are equations, but not all equations are formulas. A formula must have more than one variable. For example, $2x + 7 = y$ is an equation and a formula (it relates the unknown quantities x and y). However, $2x + 7 = 3$ is an equation but not a formula (it only expresses the value of the unknown quantity x).

Formulas are typically written with one variable alone (or isolated) on one side of the equal sign. This variable can be thought of as the subject in that the formula is stating the value of the subject in terms of the relationship between the other variables. Consider the distance formula: $distance =$

78

$rate \times time$ or $d = rt$. The value of the subject variable d (distance) is the product of the variable r and t (rate and time). Given the rate and time, the distance traveled can easily be determined by substituting the values into the formula and evaluating.

The formula $P = 2l + 2w$ expresses how to calculate the perimeter of a rectangle (P) given its length (l) and width (w). To find the perimeter of a rectangle with a length of 3ft and a width of 2ft, these values are substituted into the formula for l and w:

$$P = 2(3ft) + 2(2ft)$$

Following the order of operations, the perimeter is determined to be 10ft. When working with formulas such as these, including units is an important step.

Given a formula expressed in terms of one variable, the formula can be manipulated to express the relationship in terms of any other variable. In other words, the formula can be rearranged to change which variable is the subject. To solve for a variable of interest by manipulating a formula, the equation may be solved as if all other variables were numbers. The same steps for solving are followed, leaving operations in terms of the variables instead of calculating numerical values. For the formula $P = 2l + 2w$, the perimeter is the subject expressed in terms of the length and width. To write a formula to calculate the width of a rectangle, given its length and perimeter, the previous formula relating the three variables is solved for the variable w. If P and l were numerical values, this is a two-step linear equation solved by subtraction and division. To solve the equation $P = 2l + 2w$ for w, $2l$ is first subtracted from both sides:

$$P - 2l = 2w$$

Then both sides are divided by 2:

$$\frac{P - 2l}{2} = w$$

Function and Function Notation

A **function** is defined as a relationship between inputs and outputs where there is only one output value for a given input. As an example, the following function is in function notation:

$$f(x) = 3x - 4$$

The $f(x)$ represents the output value for an input of x. If $x = 2$, the equation becomes:

$$f(2) = 3(2) - 4 = 6 - 4 = 2$$

The input of 2 yields an output of 2, forming the ordered pair $(2, 2)$. The following set of ordered pairs corresponds to the given function: $(2, 2), (0, -4), (-2, -10)$. The set of all possible inputs of a function is its domain, and all possible outputs is called the range. By definition, each member of the domain is paired with only one member of the range.

Functions can also be defined recursively. In this form, they are not defined explicitly in terms of variables. Instead, they are defined using previously-evaluated function outputs, starting with either $f(0)$ or $f(1)$. An example of a recursively-defined function is:

$$f(1) = 2, f(n) = 2f(n - 1) + 2n, n > 1$$

The domain of this function is the set of all integers.

Functions can be built out of the context of a situation. For example, the relationship between the money paid for a gym membership and the months that someone has been a member can be described through a function. If the one-time membership fee is $40 and the monthly fee is $30, then the function can be written:

$$f(x) = 30x + 40$$

The x-value represents the number of months the person has been part of the gym, while the output is the total money paid for the membership. The table below shows this relationship. It is a representation of the function because the initial cost is $40 and the cost increases each month by $30.

x (months)	y (money paid to gym)
0	40
1	70
2	100
3	130

Functions can also be built from existing functions. For example, a given function $f(x)$ can be transformed by adding a constant, multiplying by a constant, or changing the input value by a constant. The new function $g(x) = f(x) + k$ represents a vertical shift of the original function. In $f(x) = 3x - 2$, a vertical shift 4 units up would be:

$$g(x) = 3x - 2 + 4 = 3x + 2$$

Multiplying the function times a constant k represents a vertical stretch, based on whether the constant is greater than or less than 1. The function

$$g(x) = kf(x) = 4(3x - 2) = 12x - 8$$

represents a stretch.

Changing the input x by a constant forms the function:

$$g(x) = f(x + k)$$

$$3(x + 4) - 2$$

$$3x + 12 - 2 = 3x + 10$$

and this represents a horizontal shift to the left 4 units. If $(x - 4)$ was plugged into the function, it would represent a vertical shift.

A composition function can also be formed by plugging one function into another. In function notation, this is written:

$$(f \circ g)(x) = f(g(x))$$

For two functions $f(x) = x^2$ and $g(x) = x - 3$, the composition function becomes:

$$f(g(x)) = (x - 3)^2 = x^2 - 6x + 9$$

80

The composition of functions can also be used to verify if two functions are inverses of each other. Given the two functions $f(x) = 2x + 5$ and $g(x) = \frac{x-5}{2}$, the composition function can be found $(f \circ g)(x)$. Solving this equation yields:

$$f(g(x)) = 2\left(\frac{x-5}{2}\right) + 5$$

$$x - 5 + 5 = x$$

It also is true that $g(f(x)) = x$. Since the composition of these two functions gives a simplified answer of x, this verifies that $f(x)$ and $g(x)$ are inverse functions. The domain of $f(g(x))$ is the set of all x-values in the domain of $g(x)$ such that $g(x)$ is in the domain of $f(x)$. Basically, both $f(g(x))$ and $g(x)$ have to be defined.

Functions can also be formed from combinations of existing functions.

Given $f(x)$ and $g(x)$, the following can be built:

$$f + g$$

$$f - g$$

$$fg$$

$$\frac{f}{g}$$

The domains of $f + g, f - g,$ and fg are the intersection of the domains of f and g. The domain of $\frac{f}{g}$ is the same set, excluding those values that make $g(x) = 0$.

For example, if:

$$f(x) = 2x + 3$$

$$g(x) = x + 1$$

then

$$\frac{f}{g} = \frac{2x + 3}{x + 1}$$

Its domain is all real numbers except -1.

Identifying Zeros of Polynomials

Finding the zeros of polynomial functions is the same process as finding the solutions of polynomial equations. These are the points at which the graph of the function crosses the x-axis. As stated previously, factors can be used to find the zeros of a polynomial function. The degree of the function shows the number of possible zeros. If the highest exponent on the independent variable is 4, then the degree is 4, and the number of possible zeros is 4. If there are complex solutions, the number of roots is less than the degree.

81

Given the function $y = x^2 + 7x + 6$, y can be set equal to zero, and the polynomial can be factored. The equation turns into $0 = (x + 1)(x + 6)$, where $x = -1$ and $x = -6$ are the zeros. Since this is a quadratic equation, the shape of the graph will be a parabola. Knowing that zeros represent the points where the parabola crosses the x-axis, the maximum or minimum point is the only other piece needed to sketch a rough graph of the function. By looking at the function in standard form, the coefficient of x is positive; therefore, the parabola opens up.

Using the zeros and the minimum, the following rough sketch of the graph can be constructed:

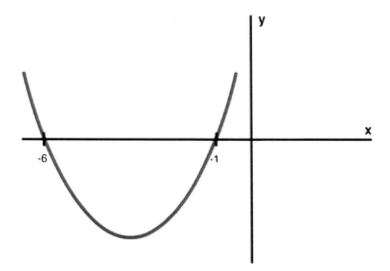

Calculating and Interpreting the Average Rate of Change

Rate of change for any line calculates the steepness of the line over a given interval. Rate of change is also known as the slope or rise/run. The rates of change for nonlinear functions vary depending on the interval being used for the function. The rate of change over one interval may be zero, while the next interval may have a positive rate of change. The equation plotted on the graph below, $y = x^2$, is a quadratic function and non-linear. The average rate of change from points $(0, 0)$ to $(1, 1)$ is 1 because the vertical change is 1 over the horizontal change of 1. For the next interval, $(1, 1)$ to $(2, 4)$, the average rate of change is 3 because the slope is $\frac{3}{1}$.

You can see that here:

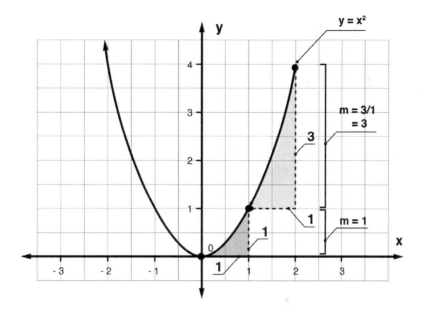

The rate of change for a linear function is constant and can be determined based on a few representations. One method is to place the equation in slope-intercept form: $y = mx + b$. Thus, m is the slope, and b is the y-intercept. In the graph below, the equation is $y = x + 1$, where the slope is 1 and the y-intercept is 1. For every vertical change of 1 unit, there is a horizontal change of 1 unit. The x-intercept is -1, which is the point where the line crosses the x-axis.

83

Probability and Statistics

Summarizing and Interpreting Data

Summarizing Data

Most statistics involve collecting a large amount of data, analyzing it, and then making decisions based on previously known information. These decisions also can be measured through additional data collection and then analyzed. Therefore, the cycle can repeat itself over and over. Representing the data visually is a large part of the process, and many plots on the real number line exist that allow this to be done. For example, a **dot plot** uses dots to represent data points above the number line. Also, a **histogram** represents a data set as a collection of rectangles, which illustrate the frequency distribution of the data. Finally, a **box plot** (also known as a box and whisker plot) plots a data set on the number line by segmenting the distribution into four quartiles that are divided equally in half by the median.

Here's an example of a box plot, a histogram, and a dot plot for the same data set:

Comparing Data

Comparing data sets within statistics can mean many things. The first way to compare data sets is by looking at the center and spread of each set. The center of a data set can mean two things: median or mean. The **median** is the value that's halfway into each data set, and it splits the data into two intervals. The **mean** is the average value of the data within a set. It's calculated by adding up all of the data in the set and dividing the total by the number of data points. Outliers can significantly impact the mean. Additionally, two completely different data sets can have the same mean. For example, a data set with values ranging from zero to 100 and a data set with values ranging from 44 to 56 can both have means of 50.

The first data set has a much wider range, which is known as the *spread* of the data. This measures how varied the data is within each set. Spread can be defined further as either interquartile range or standard deviation. The **interquartile range (IQR)** is the range of the middle 50 percent of the data set. This range can be seen in the large rectangle on a box plot. The **standard deviation (σ)** quantifies the amount of variation with respect to the mean. A lower standard deviation shows that the data set doesn't differ greatly from the mean. A larger standard deviation shows that the data set is spread out farther from the mean. The formula used for standard deviation depends on whether it's being used for a population or a sample (a subset of a population). The formula for sample standard deviation is:

$$s = \sqrt{\frac{\sum(x - \bar{x})^2}{n - 1}}$$

In this formula, s represents the standard deviation value, x is each value in the data set, $\bar{x}$ is the sample mean, and n is the total number of data points in the set. Note that sample standard deviations use *one less than the total* in the denominator. The population standard deviation formula is similar:

$$\sigma = \sqrt{\frac{\sum(x - \mu)^2}{N}}$$

For population standard deviations, sigma (σ) represents the standard deviation, x represents each value in the data set, mu (μ) is the population mean, and N is the total number of data points for the population.

Interpreting Data

The shape of a data set is another way to compare two or more sets of data. If a data set isn't symmetric around its mean, it's said to be *skewed*. If the tail to the left of the mean is longer, it's said to be skewed to the left. In this case, the mean is less than the median. Conversely, if the tail to the right of the mean is longer, it's said to be skewed to the right and the mean is greater than the median. When classifying a data set according to its shape, its overall skewness is being discussed. If the mean and median are equal, the data set isn't *skewed*; it is *symmetric*, and is considered normally distributed.

An **outlier** is a data point that lies a great distance away from the majority of the data set. It also can be labelled as an extreme value. Technically, an outlier is any value that falls 1.5 times the IQR above the upper quartile or 1.5 times the IQR below the lower quartile. The effect of outliers in the data set is seen visually because they affect the mean. If there's a large difference between the mean and mode, outliers are the cause. The mean shows bias towards the outlying values. However, the median won't be affected as greatly by outliers.

Using Measures of Center to Draw Inferences About Populations

The center of a set of data (statistical values) can be represented by its mean, median, or mode. These are sometimes referred to as measures of central tendency.

Mean

The first property that can be defined for this set of data is the mean. This is the same as the average. To find the mean, add up all the data points, then divide by the total number of data points. For example, suppose that in a class of 10 students, the scores on a test were 50, 60, 65, 65, 75, 80, 85, 85, 90, 100. Therefore, the average test score will be:

$$\frac{50 + 60 + 65 + 65 + 75 + 80 + 85 + 85 + 90 + 100}{10} = 75.5$$

The mean is a useful number if the distribution of data is normal which roughly means that the frequency of different outcomes has a single peak and is roughly equally distributed on both sides of that peak. However, it is less useful in some cases where the data might be split or where there are some outliers. Outliers are data points that are far from the rest of the data. For example, suppose there are 10 executives and 90 employees at a company. The executives make $1,000 per hour, and the employees make $10 per hour.

Therefore, the average pay rate will be:

$$\frac{\$1,000 \times 10 + \$10 \times 90}{100} = \$109 \text{ per hour}$$

In this case, this average is not very descriptive since it's not close to the actual pay of the executives or the employees.

Median

Another useful measurement is the median. In a data set, the median is the point in the middle. The middle refers to the point where half the data comes before it and half comes after, when the data is recorded in numerical order. For instance, these are the speeds of the fastball of a pitcher during the last inning that he pitched (in order from least to greatest):

$$90, 92, 93, 93, 95, 96, 97, 97, 97$$

There are nine total numbers, so the middle or median number is the 5th one, which is 95.

In cases where the number of data points is an even number, then the average of the two middle points is taken. In the previous example of test scores, the two middle points are 75 and 80. Since there is no single point, the average of these two scores needs to be found. The average is:

$$\frac{75 + 80}{2} = 77.5$$

The median is generally a good value to use if there are a few outliers in the data. It prevents those outliers from affecting the "middle" value as much as when using the mean.

Since an outlier is a data point that is far from most of the other data points in a data set, this means an outlier also is any point that is far from the median of the data set. The outliers can have a substantial effect on the mean of a data set, but they usually do not change the median or mode, or do not change them by a large quantity. For example, consider the data set (3, 5, 6, 6, 6, 8). This has a median of 6 and a mode of 6, with a mean of $\frac{34}{6} \approx 5.67$. Now, suppose a new data point of 1,000 is added so that the data set is now (3, 5, 6, 6, 6, 8, 1,000). The median and mode, which are both still 6, remain unchanged. However, the average is now $\frac{1,034}{7}$, which is approximately 147.7. In this case, the median and mode will be better descriptions for most of the data points.

Outliers in a given data set are sometimes the result of an error by the experimenter, but oftentimes, they are perfectly valid data points that must be taken into consideration.

Mode
One additional measure to define for X is the mode. This is the data point that appears most frequently. If two or more data points all tie for the most frequent appearance, then each of them is considered a mode. In the case of the test scores, where the numbers were 50, 60, 65, 65, 75, 80, 85, 85, 90, 100, there are two modes: 65 and 85.

Using Statistics to Gain Information About a Population

Statistics involves making decisions and predictions about larger data sets based on smaller data sets. Basically, the information from one part or subset can help predict what happens in the entire data set or population at large. The entire process involves guessing, and the predictions and decisions may not be 100 percent correct all of the time; however, there is some truth to these predictions, and the decisions do have mathematical support. The smaller data set is called a **sample** and the larger data set (in which the decision is being made) is called a **population.** A random sample is used as the sample, which is an unbiased collection of data points that represents the population as well as it can. There are many methods of forming a random sample, and all adhere to the fact that every potential data point has a predetermined probability of being chosen. Statistical inference, based in probability theory, makes calculated assumptions about an entire population based on data from a sample set from that population.

A population is the entire set of people or things of interest. Suppose a study is intended to determine the number of hours of sleep per night for college females in the U.S. The population would consist of every college female in the country. A sample is a subset of the population that may be used for the study. It would not be practical to survey every female college student, so a sample might consist of 100 students per school from 20 different colleges in the country. From the results of the survey, a sample statistic can be calculated. A sample statistic is a numerical characteristic of the sample data, including mean and variance. A sample statistic can be used to estimate a corresponding population parameter. A population parameter is a numerical characteristic of the entire population. Suppose the sample data had a mean (average) of 5.5. This sample statistic can be used as an estimate of the population parameter (average hours of sleep for every college female in the U.S.).

Representing Data

Chart is a broad term that refers to a variety of ways to represent data.

To graph relations, the **Cartesian plane** is used. This means to think of the plane as being given a grid of squares, with one direction being the *x*-axis and the other direction the *y*-axis. Generally, the independent variable is placed along the horizontal axis, and the dependent variable is placed along the vertical axis. Any point on the plane can be specified by saying how far to go along the *x*-axis and how far along the *y*-axis with a pair of numbers (x, y). Specific values for these pairs can be given names such as $C = (-1, 3)$. Negative values mean to move left or down; positive values mean to move right or up. The point where the axes cross one another is called the **origin**. The origin has coordinates $(0, 0)$ and is usually called O when given a specific label. An illustration of the Cartesian plane, along with the plotted points $(2, 1)$ and $(-1, -1)$, is below.

A **line plot** is a diagram that shows quantity of data along a number line. It is a quick way to record data in a structure similar to a bar graph without needing to do the required shading of a bar graph. Here is an example of a line plot:

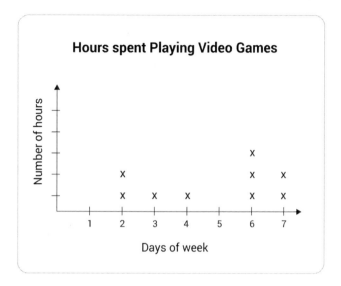

A **tally chart** is a diagram in which tally marks are utilized to represent data. Tally marks are a means of showing a quantity of objects within a specific classification. Here is an example of a tally chart:

Number of days with rain	Number of weeks
0	II
1	IIII
2	IIII
3	IIII
4	IIII IIII IIII IIII
5	IIII I
6	IIII I
7	IIII

Data is often recorded using fractions, such as half a mile, and understanding fractions is critical because of their popular use in real-world applications. Also, it is extremely important to label values with their units when using data. For example, regarding length, the number 2 is meaningless unless it is attached to a unit. Writing 2 cm shows that the number refers to the length of an object.

A **picture graph** is a diagram that shows pictorial representation of data being discussed. The symbols used can represent a certain number of objects. Notice how each fruit symbol in the following graph represents a count of two fruits. One drawback of picture graphs is that they can be less accurate if each symbol represents a large number. For example, if each banana symbol represented ten bananas, and students consumed 22 bananas, it may be challenging to draw and interpret two and one-fifth bananas as a frequency count of 22.

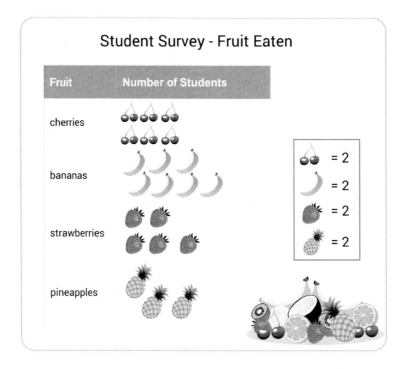

A **circle graph**, also called a pie chart, shows categorical data with each category representing a percentage of the whole data set. To make a circle graph, the percent of the data set for each category must be determined. To do so, the frequency of the category is divided by the total number of data points and converted to a percent. For example, if 80 people were asked what their favorite sport is and 20 responded basketball, basketball makes up 25% of the data:

$$\frac{20}{80} = 0.25 = 25\%$$

Each category in a data set is represented by a *slice* of the circle proportionate to its percentage of the whole.

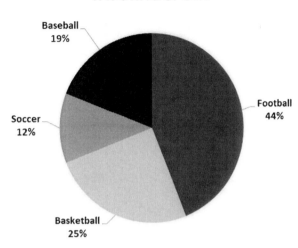

FAVORITE SPORT

A **scatter plot** displays the relationship between two variables. Values for the independent variable, typically denoted by *x*, are paired with values for the dependent variable, typically denoted by *y*. Each set of corresponding values are written as an ordered pair (*x*, *y*). To construct the graph, a coordinate grid is labeled with the *x*-axis representing the independent variable and the *y*-axis representing the dependent variable. Each ordered pair is graphed.

Like a scatter plot, a **line graph** compares two variables that change continuously, typically over time. Paired data values (ordered pair) are plotted on a coordinate grid with the *x*- and *y*-axis representing the two variables. A line is drawn from each point to the next, going from left to right. A double line graph simply displays two sets of data that contain values for the same two variables. The double line graph below displays the profit for given years (two variables) for Company A and Company B (two data sets).

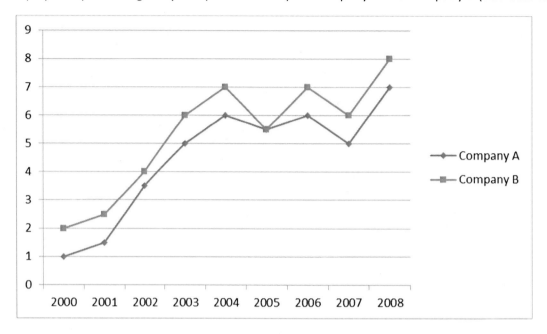

Choosing the appropriate graph to display a data set depends on what type of data is included in the set and what information must be shown.

Scatter plots and line graphs can be used to display data consisting of two variables. Examples include height and weight, or distance and time. A correlation between the variables is determined by examining the points on the graph. Line graphs are used if each value for one variable pairs with a distinct value for the other variable. Line graphs show relationships between variables.

Approximating the Probability of a Chance Event

Probability is a measure of how likely an event is to occur. Probability is written as a fraction between zero and one. If an event has a probability of zero, the event will never occur. If an event has a probability of one, the event will definitely occur. If the probability of an event is closer to zero, the event is unlikely to occur. If the probability of an event is closer to one, the event is more likely to occur. For example, a probability of $\frac{1}{2}$ means that the event is equally as likely to occur as it is not to occur. An example of this is tossing a coin. The probability of an event can be calculated by dividing the number of favorable outcomes by the number of total outcomes. For example, suppose you have 2 raffle tickets out of 20 total tickets sold. The probability that you win the raffle is calculated:

$$\frac{number\ of\ favorable\ outcomes}{total\ number of\ outcomes} = \frac{2}{20} = \frac{1}{10}$$

(always reduce fractions). Therefore, the probability of winning the raffle is $\frac{1}{10}$ or 0.1.

Chance is the measure of how likely an event is to occur, written as a percent. If an event will never occur, the event has a 0% chance. If an event will certainly occur, the event has a 100% chance. If an

92

event will sometimes occur, the event has a chance somewhere between 0% and 100%. To calculate chance, probability is calculated, and the fraction is converted to a percent.

The probability of multiple events occurring can be determined by multiplying the probability of each event. For example, suppose you flip a coin with heads and tails, and roll a six-sided dice numbered one through six. To find the probability that you will flip heads AND roll a two, the probability of each event is determined, and those fractions are multiplied. The probability of flipping heads is:

$$\frac{1}{2}\left(\frac{1 \ side \ with \ heads}{2 \ sides \ total}\right)$$

and the probability of rolling a two is:

$$\frac{1}{6}\left(\frac{1 \ side \ with \ a \ 2}{6 \ total \ sides}\right)$$

The probability of flipping heads AND rolling a 2 is:

$$\frac{1}{2} \times \frac{1}{6} = \frac{1}{12}$$

The above scenario with flipping a coin and rolling a dice is an example of independent events. Independent events are circumstances in which the outcome of one event does not affect the outcome of the other event. Conversely, dependent events are ones in which the outcome of one event affects the outcome of the second event. Consider the following scenario: a bag contains 5 black marbles and 5 white marbles. What is the probability of picking 2 black marbles without replacing the marble after the first pick?

The probability of picking a black marble on the first pick is:

$$\frac{5}{10}\left(\frac{5 \ black \ marbles}{10 \ total \ marbles}\right)$$

Assuming that a black marble was picked, there are now 4 black marbles and 5 white marbles for the second pick. Therefore, the probability of picking a black marble on the second pick is:

$$\frac{4}{9}\left(\frac{4 \ black \ marbles}{9 \ total \ marbles}\right)$$

To find the probability of picking two black marbles, the probability of each is multiplied:

$$\frac{5}{10} \times \frac{4}{9} = \frac{20}{90} = \frac{2}{9}$$

Probabilities of Single and Compound Events

A **simple event** consists of only one outcome. The most popular simple event is flipping a coin, which results in either heads or tails. A **compound event** results in more than one outcome and consists of more than one simple event. An example of a compound event is flipping a coin while tossing a die. The result is either heads or tails on the coin and a number from one to six on the die. The probability of a simple event is calculated by dividing the number of possible outcomes by the total number of outcomes. Therefore, the probability of obtaining heads on a coin is $\frac{1}{2}$, and the probability of rolling a 6 on a die is $\frac{1}{6}$. The probability of compound events is calculated using the basic idea of the probability of simple events. If the two events are independent, the probability of one outcome is equal to the product of the probabilities of each simple event. For example, the probability of obtaining heads on a coin and rolling a 6 is equal to:

$$\frac{1}{2} \times \frac{1}{6} = \frac{1}{12}$$

The probability of either A or B occurring is equal to the sum of the probabilities minus the probability that both A and B will occur. Therefore, the probability of obtaining either heads on a coin or rolling a 6 on a die is:

$$\frac{1}{2} + \frac{1}{6} - \frac{1}{12} = \frac{7}{12}$$

The two events aren't mutually exclusive because they can happen at the same time. If two events are mutually exclusive, and the probability of both events occurring at the same time is zero, the probability of event A or B occurring equals the sum of both probabilities. An example of calculating the probability of two mutually exclusive events is determining the probability of pulling a king or a queen from a deck of cards. The two events cannot occur at the same time.

Geometry and Measurements

Using Congruence and Similarity Criteria for Triangles

To prove theorems about triangles, basic definitions involving triangles (e.g., equilateral, isosceles, etc.) need to be known. Proven theorems concerning lines and angles can be applied to prove theorems about triangles. Common theorems to be proved include: the sum of all angles in a triangle equals 180 degrees; the sum of the lengths of two sides of a triangle is greater than the length of the third side; the base angles of an isosceles triangle are congruent; the line segment connecting the midpoint of two sides of a triangle is parallel to the third side and its length is half the length of the third side; and the medians of a triangle all meet at a single point.

Triangle Congruence

There are five theorems to show that triangles are congruent when it's unknown whether each pair of angles and sides are congruent. Each theorem is a shortcut that involves different combinations of sides and angles that must be true for the two triangles to be congruent.

For example, **side-side-side (SSS)** states that if all sides are equal, the triangles are congruent. **Side-angle-side (SAS)** states that if two pairs of sides are equal and the included angles are congruent, then the triangles are congruent. Similarly, **angle-side-angle (ASA)** states that if two pairs of angles are congruent and the included side lengths are equal, the triangles are similar. **Angle-angle-side (AAS)** states that two triangles are congruent if they have two pairs of congruent angles and a pair of corresponding equal side lengths that aren't included. Finally, **hypotenuse-leg (HL)** states that if two right triangles have equal hypotenuses and an equal pair of shorter sides, then the triangles are congruent.

An important item to note is that angle-angle-angle *(AAA)* is not enough information to have congruence. It's important to understand why these rules work by using rigid motions to show

94

congruence between the triangles with the given properties. For example, three reflections are needed to show why *SAS* follows from the definition of congruence.

Similarity for Two Triangles

If two angles of one triangle are congruent with two angles of a second triangle, the triangles are similar. This is because, within any triangle, the sum of the angle measurements is 180 degrees. Therefore, if two are congruent, the third angle must also be congruent because their measurements are equal. Three congruent pairs of angles mean that the triangles are similar.

Proving Congruence and Similarity

The criteria needed to prove triangles are congruent involves both angle and side congruence. Both pairs of related angles and sides need to be of the same measurement to use congruence in a proof. The criteria to prove similarity in triangles involves proportionality of side lengths. Angles must be congruent in similar triangles; however, corresponding side lengths only need to be a constant multiple of each other. Once similarity is established, it can be used in proofs as well. Relationships in geometric figures other than triangles can be proven using triangle congruence and similarity. If a similar or congruent triangle can be found within another type of geometric figure, their criteria can be used to prove a relationship about a given formula. For example, a rectangle can be broken up into two congruent triangles.

Properties of Polygons and Circles

A **polygon** is a closed two-dimensional figure consisting of three or more sides. Polygons can be either convex or concave. A polygon that has interior angles all measuring less than 180° is convex. A concave polygon has one or more interior angles measuring greater than 180°. Examples are shown below.

Polygons can be classified by the number of sides (also equal to the number of angles) they have. The following are the names of polygons with a given number of sides or angles:

# of Sides	Name of Polygon
Triangle	3
Quadrilateral	4
Pentagon	5
Hexagon	6
Septagon (or heptagon)	7
Octagon	8
Nonagon	9
Decagon	10

Equiangular polygons are polygons in which the measure of every interior angle is the same. The sides of equilateral polygons are always the same length. If a polygon is both equiangular and equilateral, the polygon is defined as a regular polygon. Examples are shown below.

97

Triangles can be further classified by their sides and angles. A triangle with its largest angle measuring 90° is a right triangle.

Right triangle

A triangle with the largest angle less than 90° is an acute triangle. A triangle with the largest angle greater than 90° is an obtuse triangle.

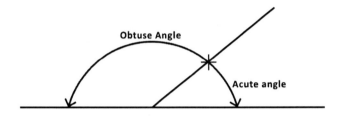

A triangle consisting of two equal sides and two equal angles is an isosceles triangle. A triangle with three equal sides and three equal angles is an equilateral triangle. A triangle with no equal sides or angles is a scalene triangle.

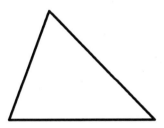

Equilateral Triangle   **Isosceles Triangle**   **Scalene Triangle**

Quadrilaterals can be further classified according to their sides and angles. A quadrilateral with exactly one pair of parallel sides is called a **trapezoid**. A quadrilateral that shows both pairs of opposite sides parallel is a **parallelogram**. Parallelograms include rhombuses, rectangles, and squares. A rhombus has four equal sides. A rectangle has four equal angles (90° each). A square has four 90° angles and four equal sides. Therefore, a square is both a rhombus and a rectangle.

Use this chart for a better understanding of quadrilaterals:

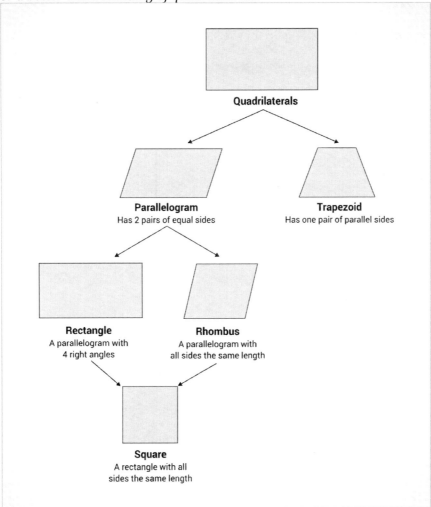

There are many key facts related to geometry that are applicable. The sum of the measures of the angles of a triangle are 180°, and for a quadrilateral, the sum is 360°. Rectangles and squares each have four right angles. A right angle has a measure of 90°.

A parallelogram has six important properties:

- Opposite sides are congruent.
- Opposite angles are congruent.
- Within a parallelogram, consecutive angles are supplementary, so their measurements total 180 degrees.
- If one angle is a right angle, all of them have to be right angles.
- The diagonals of the angles bisect each other.
- These diagonals form two congruent triangles.

Perimeter and Area

The **perimeter** is the distance around a figure or the sum of all sides of a polygon.

The formula for the perimeter of a square is four times the length of a side. For example, the following square has side lengths of 5 meters:

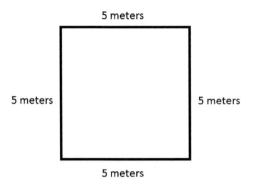

The perimeter is 20 meters because 4 times 5 is 20.

The formula for a perimeter of a rectangle is the sum of twice the length and twice the width. For example, if the length of a rectangle is 10 inches and the width 8 inches, then the perimeter is 36 inches because:

$$P = 2l + 2w = 2(10) + 2(8) = 20 + 16 = 36 \text{ inches}$$

The **circumference** of a circle is found by calculating the perimeter of the shape. The ratio of the circumference to the diameter of the circle is π, so the formula for circumference is:

$$C = \pi d = 2\pi r$$

The **area** is the amount of space inside of a figure, and there are formulas associated with area.

The area of a triangle is the product of ½ the base and height. For example, if the base of the triangle is 2 feet and the height is 4 feet, then the area is 4 square feet. The following equation shows the formula used to calculate the area of the triangle:

$$A = \frac{1}{2}bh = \frac{1}{2}(2)(4) = 4 \text{ square feet}$$

The area of a square is the length of a side squared. For example, if a side of a square is 7 centimeters, then the area is 49 square centimeters. The formula for this example is $A = s^2 = 7^2 = 49$ square centimeters. An example is if the rectangle has a length of 6 inches and a width of 7 inches, then the area is 42 square inches:

$$A = lw = 6(7) = 42 \text{ square inches}$$

The area of a trapezoid is ½ the height times the sum of the bases. For example, if the length of the bases are 2.5 and 3 feet and the height 3.5 feet, then the area is 9.625 square feet. The following formula shows how the area is calculated:

$$A = \frac{1}{2}h(b_1 + b_2)$$

$$\frac{1}{2}(3.5)(2.5 + 3)$$

$$\frac{1}{2}(3.5)(5.5)$$

$$9.625 \text{ square feet}$$

The perimeter of a figure is measured in single units, while the area is measured in square units.

Surface Area and Volume Formulas

Surface area and volume are two- and three-dimensional measurements. **Surface area** measures the total surface space of an object, like the six sides of a cube. Questions about surface area will ask how much of something is needed to cover a three-dimensional object, like wrapping a present. **Volume** is the measurement of how much space an object occupies, like how much space is in the cube. Volume questions will ask how much of something is needed to completely fill the object. The most common surface area and volume questions deal with spheres, cubes, and rectangular prisms.

The formula for a cube's surface area is $SA = 6 \times s^2$, where s is the length of a side. A cube has 6 equal sides, so the formula expresses the area of all the sides. Volume is simply measured by taking the cube of the length, so the formula is $V = s^3$.

The surface area formula for a rectangular prism or a general box is:

$$SA = 2(lw + lh + wh)$$

l is the length, h is the height, and w is the width. The volume formula is $V = l \times w \times h$, which is the cube's volume formula adjusted for the unequal lengths of a box's sides.

The formula for a sphere's surface area is $SA = 4\pi r^2$, where r is the sphere's radius. The surface area formula is the area for a circle multiplied by four. To measure volume, the formula is:

$$V = \frac{4}{3}\pi r^3$$

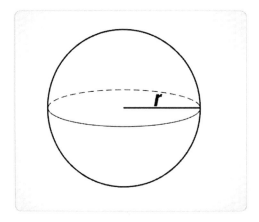

A rectangular pyramid is a figure with a rectangular base and four triangular sides that meet at a single vertex. If the rectangle has sides of lengths x and y, then the volume will be given by:

$$V = \frac{1}{3}xyh$$

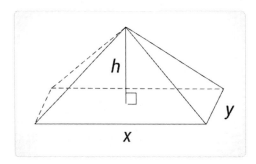

To find the surface area, the dimensions of each triangle must be known. However, these dimensions can differ depending on the problem in question.

Therefore, there is no general formula for calculating total surface area.

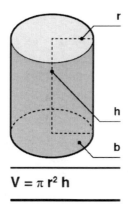

$$V = \pi\, r^2\, h$$

The formula to find the volume of a cylinder is $\pi r^2 h$. This formula contains the formula for the area of a circle (πr^2) because the base of a cylinder is a circle. To calculate the volume of a cylinder, the slices of circles needed to build the entire height of the cylinder are added together. For example, if the radius is 5 feet and the height of the cylinder is 10 feet, the cylinder's volume is calculated by using the following equation: $\pi 5^2 \times 10$. Substituting 3.14 for π, the volume is 785 ft³.

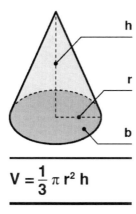

$$V = \frac{1}{3}\, \pi\, r^2\, h$$

The formula used to calculate the volume of a cone is $\frac{1}{3}\pi r^2 h$. Essentially, the area of the base of the cone is multiplied by the cone's height. In a real-life example where the radius of a cone is 2 meters and the height of a cone is 5 meters, the volume of the cone is calculated by utilizing the formula:

$$\frac{1}{3}\pi 2^2 \times 5$$

After substituting 3.14 for π, the volume is 20.9 m³.

Angles and Measurement

Supplementary angles add up to 180 degrees. **Vertical angles** are two nonadjacent angles formed by two intersecting lines. For example, in the following picture, angles 4 and 2 are vertical angles and so are angles 1 and 3:

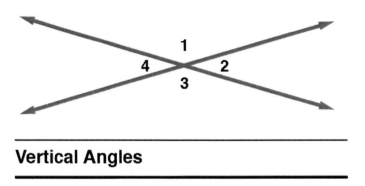

Vertical Angles

Corresponding angles are two angles in the same position whenever a straight line (known as a transversal) crosses two others. If the two lines are parallel, the corresponding angles are equal. In the following diagram, angles 1 and 3 are corresponding angles but aren't equal to each other:

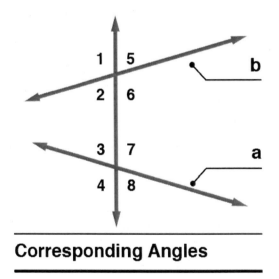

Corresponding Angles

Alternate interior angles are also a pair of angles formed when two lines are crossed by a transversal. They are opposite angles that exist inside of the two lines. In the corresponding angles diagram above, angles 2 and 7 are alternate interior angles, as well as angles 6 and 3. **Alternate exterior angles** are opposite angles formed by a transversal but, in contrast to interior angles, exterior angles exist outside the two original lines. Therefore, angles 1 and 8 are alternate exterior angles and so are angles 5 and 4. Finally, **consecutive interior angles** are pairs of angles formed by a transversal. These angles are located

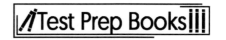

on the same side of the transversal and inside the two original lines. Therefore, angles 2 and 3 are a pair of consecutive interior angles, and so are angles 6 and 7. These definitions are instrumental in solving many problems that involve determining relationships between angles.

The Pythagorean Theorem

The **Pythagorean theorem** is an important relationship between the three sides of a right triangle. It states that the square of the side opposite the right triangle, known as the **hypotenuse** (denoted as c^2), is equal to the sum of the squares of the other two sides ($a^2 + b^2$). Thus,

$$a^2 + b^2 = c^2$$

The theorem can be seen in the following image:

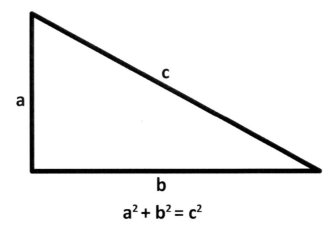

$$a^2 + b^2 = c^2$$

Both the trigonometric functions and the Pythagorean theorem can be used in problems that involve finding either a missing side or a missing angle of a right triangle. To do so, one must look to see what sides and angles are given and select the correct relationship that will help find the missing value. These relationships can also be used to solve application problems involving right triangles. Often, it's helpful to draw a figure to represent the problem to see what's missing.

As an example of the theorem, suppose that Shirley has a rectangular field that is 5 feet wide and 12 feet long, and she wants to split it in half using a fence that goes from one corner to the opposite corner. How long will this fence need to be? To figure this out, note that this makes the field into two right triangles, whose hypotenuse will be the fence dividing it in half. Therefore, the fence length is given by:

$$\sqrt{5^2 + 12^2} = \sqrt{169} = 13 \text{ feet long}$$

Transformations in the Plane

Transformations in the Plane
A **transformation** occurs when a shape is altered in the plane where it exists. There are three major types of transformation: translations, reflections, and rotations. A **translation** consists of shifting a shape in one direction. A **reflection** results when a shape is transformed over a line to its mirror image. Finally, a **rotation** occurs when a shape moves in a circular motion around a specified point. The object can be turned clockwise or counterclockwise and, if rotated 360 degrees, returns to its original location.

Distance and Angle Measure

The three major types of transformations preserve distance and angle measurement. The shapes stay the same, but they are moved to another place in the plane. Therefore, the distance between any two points on the shape doesn't change. Also, any original angle measure between two line segments doesn't change. However, there are transformations that don't preserve distance and angle measurements, including those that don't preserve the original shape. For example, transformations that involve stretching and shrinking shapes don't preserve distance and angle measures. In these cases, the input variables are multiplied by either a number greater than one (stretch) or less than one (shrink).

Rigid Motion

A **rigid motion** is a transformation that preserves distance and length. Every line segment in the resulting image is congruent to the corresponding line segment in the pre-image. Congruence between two figures means a series of transformations (or a rigid motion) can be defined that maps one of the figures onto the other. Basically, two figures are congruent if they have the same shape and size.

Dilation

A shape is dilated, or a **dilation** occurs, when each side of the original image is multiplied by a given scale factor. If the scale factor is less than 1 and greater than 0, the dilation contracts the shape and the resulting shape is smaller. If the scale factor equals 1, the resulting shape is the same size and the dilation is a rigid motion. Finally, if the scale factor is greater than 1, the resulting shape is larger and the dilation expands the shape. The center of dilation is the point where the distance from it to any point on the new shape equals the scale factor times the distance from the center to the corresponding point in the pre-image. Dilation isn't an isometric transformation because distance isn't preserved. However, angle measure, parallel lines, and points on a line all remain unchanged. This following figure is an example of translation, rotation, dilation, and reflection:

Determining Congruence

Two figures are congruent if there is a rigid motion that can map one figure onto the other. Therefore, all pairs of sides and angles within the image and pre-image must be congruent. For example, in triangles, each pair of the three sides and three angles must be congruent. Similarly, in two four-sided figures, each pair of the four sides and four angles must be congruent.

Properties of Lines

In geometry, a line connects two points, has no thickness, and extends indefinitely in both directions beyond each point. If the length is finite, it's known as a line segment and has two endpoints. A ray is the straight portion of a line that has one endpoint and extends indefinitely in the other direction. An angle is formed when two rays begin at the same endpoint and extend indefinitely. The endpoint of an angle is called a vertex. Adjacent angles are two side-by-side angles formed from the same ray that have the same endpoint. Angles are measured in degrees or radians, which is a measure of rotation. A full rotation equals 360 degrees or 2π radians, which represents a circle. Half a rotation equals 180 degrees or π radians and represents a half-circle. Subsequently, 90 degrees ($\frac{\pi}{2}$ radians) represents a quarter of a circle, which is known as a right angle. Any angle less than 90 degrees is an acute angle, and any angle greater than 90 degrees is an obtuse angle. Angle measurement is additive. When an angle is broken into two non-overlapping angles, the total measure of the larger angle equals the sum of the two smaller angles. Lines are coplanar if they're located in the same plane. Two lines are parallel if they are coplanar, extend in the same direction, and never cross. If lines do cross, they're labeled as intersecting lines because they "intersect" at one point. If they intersect at more than one point, they're the same line. Perpendicular lines are coplanar lines that form a right angle at their point of intersection.

Two lines are parallel if they have the same slope and a different intercept. Two lines are perpendicular if the product of their slope equals -1. Parallel lines never intersect unless they are the same line, and perpendicular lines intersect at a right angle. If two lines aren't parallel, they must intersect at one point. Determining equations of lines based on properties of parallel and perpendicular lines appears in word problems. To find an equation of a line, both the slope and a point the line goes through are necessary. Therefore, if an equation of a line is needed that's parallel to a given line and runs through a specified point, the slope of the given line and the point are plugged into the point-slope form of an equation of a line. Secondly, if an equation of a line is needed that's perpendicular to a given line running through a specified point, the negative reciprocal of the slope of the given line and the point are plugged into the point-slope form. Also, if the point of intersection of two lines is known, that point will be used to solve the set of equations. Therefore, to solve a system of equations, the point of intersection must be found. If a set of two equations with two unknown variables has no solution, the lines are parallel.

SHSAT Practice Test #1

Editing/Revising

Editing/Revising Part A

1. Read this sentence.

> Protestors filled the streets of the city. Because they were dissatisfied with the government's leadership.

How should this sentence be revised?

    a. Protestors filled the streets of the city, because they were dissatisfied with the government's leadership.
    b. Protesters, filled the streets of the city, because they were dissatisfied with the government's leadership.
    c. Because they were dissatisfied with the government's leadership protestors filled the streets of the city.
    d. Protestors filled the streets of the city because they were dissatisfied with the government's leadership.

2. Read this sentence.

> She's looking for a suitcase that can fit all of her clothes, shoes, accessory, and makeup.

How should the sentence be revised?

    e. Change *shoes* to **shoe**.
    f. Change the commas to semicolons.
    g. Change *makeup* to **makeups**.
    h. Change *accessory* to **accessories**.

3. Read this paragraph.

> (1) Early in my career, a master's teacher shared this thought with me: "Education is the last bastion of civility." (2) While I did not completely understand the scope of those words at the time, I have since come to realize the depth, breadth, truth, and significance of what he said. (3) Education provides society with a vehicle for raising it's children to be civil, decent, human beings with something valuable to contribute to the world. (4) It is really what makes us human and what distinguishes us as civilized creatures.

How should the paragraph be revised?

    a. Sentence 1: Move the period to outside the quotation marks.
    b. Sentence 2: Remove the comma after *time*.
    c. Sentence 3: Remove the apostrophe from *it's*.
    d. Sentence 4: Change *distinguishes* to **distinguished**.

4. Read this paragraph.

> (1) George Washington Carver was an innovator, always thinking of new and better ways to do things and is most famous for his over three hundred uses for the peanut. (2) Toward the end of his career, Carver returns to his first love of art. (3) When Carver died, he left his money to help fund ongoing agricultural research. (4) Today, people still visit and study at the George Washington Carver Foundation at the Tuskegee Institute.

Which sentence contains an error in construction and should be revised?
- e. Sentence 1
- f. Sentence 2
- g. Sentence 3
- h. Sentence 4

Editing/Revising Part B

Questions 5–19 are based on the following passage:

> The knowledge of an aircraft engineer is acquired through years of education, and special (1) <u>licenses are required</u>. Ideally, an individual will begin their preparation for the profession in high school (2) <u>by taking chemistry physics trigonometry and calculus.</u> Such curricula will aid in (3) <u>one's pursuit of a bachelor's degree</u> in aircraft engineering, which requires several physical and life sciences, mathematics, and design courses.
>
> (4) <u>Some of universities provide internship or apprentice opportunities</u> for the students enrolled in aircraft engineer programs. A bachelor's in aircraft engineering is commonly accompanied by a master's degree in advanced engineering or business administration. Such advanced degrees enable an individual to position himself or herself for executive, faculty, and/or research opportunities. (5) <u>These advanced offices oftentimes require a Professional Engineering (PE) license which can be obtained through additional college courses, professional experience, and acceptable scores on the Fundamentals of Engineering (FE) and Professional Engineering (PE) standardized assessments.</u>
>
> (6) <u>Once the job begins, this lines of work</u> requires critical thinking, business skills, problem solving, and creativity. This level of (7) <u>expertise</u> (8) <u>allows</u> aircraft engineers to (9) <u>apply mathematical equation and scientific processes</u> to aeronautical and aerospace issues or inventions. (10) <u>For example,</u> aircraft engineers may test, design, and construct flying vessels such as airplanes, space shuttles, and missile weapons. As a result, aircraft engineers are compensated with generous salaries. In fact, in May 2014, the lowest 10 percent of all American aircraft engineers earned less than $60,110 while the highest paid ten-percent of all American aircraft engineers earned $155,240. (11) <u>In May 2015, the United States Bureau of Labor Statistics (BLS) reported that the median annual salary of aircraft engineers was $107,830.</u> (12) <u>Conversely,</u> (13) <u>employment opportunities for aircraft engineers are projected to decrease by 2 percent by 2024.</u> This decrease may be the result of a decline in the manufacturing industry. (14) <u>Nevertheless aircraft engineers who know how to utilize</u> modeling and simulation programs, fluid dynamic software, and robotic engineering tools (15) <u>is projected to remain</u> the most employable.

5. Which of the following would be the best choice for this sentence (reproduced below)?

> The knowledge of an aircraft engineer is acquired through years of education, and special (1) <u>licenses are required</u>.

a. NO CHANGE
b. licenses will be required
c. licenses may be required
d. licenses should be required

6. Which of the following would be the best choice for this sentence (reproduced below)?

> Ideally, an individual will begin their preparation for the profession in high school (2) <u>by taking chemistry physics trigonometry and calculus.</u>

e. NO CHANGE
f. by taking chemistry; physics; trigonometry; and calculus.
g. by taking chemistry, physics, trigonometry, and calculus.
h. by taking chemistry, physics, trigonometry, calculus.

7. Which of the following would be the best choice for this sentence (reproduced below)?

> Such curricula will aid in (3) <u>one's pursuit of a bachelor's degree</u> in aircraft engineering, which requires several physical and life sciences, mathematics, and design courses.

a. NO CHANGE
b. ones pursuit of a bachelors degree
c. one's pursuit of a bachelors degree
d. ones pursuit of a bachelor's degree

8. Which of the following would be the best choice for this sentence (reproduced below)?

> (4) <u>Some of universities provide internship or apprentice opportunities</u> for the students enrolled in aircraft engineer programs.

e. NO CHANGE
f. Some of universities provided internship or apprentice opportunities
g. Some of universities provide internship or apprenticeship opportunities
h. Some universities provide internship or apprenticeship opportunities

9. Which of the following would be the best choice for this sentence (reproduced below)?

(5) <u>These advanced offices oftentimes require a Professional Engineering (PE) license which can be obtained through additional college courses, professional experience, and acceptable scores on the Fundamentals of Engineering (FE) and Professional Engineering (PE) standardized assessments.</u>

a. NO CHANGE
b. These advanced positions oftentimes require acceptable scores on the Fundamentals of Engineering (FE) and Professional Engineering (PE) standardized assessments in order to achieve a Professional Engineering (PE) license. Additional college courses and professional experience help.
c. These advanced offices oftentimes require acceptable scores on the Fundamentals of Engineering (FE) and Professional Engineering (PE) standardized assessments to gain the Professional Engineering (PE) license which can be obtained through additional college courses, professional experience.
d. These advanced positions oftentimes require a Professional Engineering (PE) license which is obtained by acceptable scores on the Fundamentals of Engineering (FE) and Professional Engineering (PE) standardized assessments. Further education and professional experience can help prepare for the assessments.

10. Which of the following would be the best choice for this sentence (reproduced below)?

(6) <u>Once the job begins, this lines of work</u> requires critical thinking, business skills, problem solving, and creativity.

e. NO CHANGE
f. Once the job begins, this line of work
g. Once the job begins, these line of work
h. Once the job begin, this line of work

11. Which of the following would be the best choice for this sentence (reproduced below)?

This level of (7) <u>expertise</u> allows aircraft engineers to apply mathematical equation and scientific processes to aeronautical and aerospace issues or inventions.

a. NO CHANGE
b. expertis
c. expirtise
d. excpertise

12. Which of the following would be the best choice for this sentence (reproduced below)?

> This level of expertise (8) <u>allows</u> aircraft engineers to apply mathematical equation and scientific processes to aeronautical and aerospace issues or inventions.

- e. NO CHANGE
- f. Inhibits
- g. Requires
- h. Should

13. Which of the following would be the best choice for this sentence (reproduced below)?

> This level of expertise allows aircraft engineers to (9) <u>apply mathematical equation and scientific processes</u> to aeronautical and aerospace issues or inventions.

- a. NO CHANGE
- b. apply mathematical equations and scientific process
- c. apply mathematical equation and scientific process
- d. apply mathematical equations and scientific processes

14. Which of the following would be the best choice for this sentence (reproduced below)?

> (10) <u>For example,</u> aircraft engineers may test, design, and construct flying vessels such as airplanes, space shuttles, and missile weapons.

- e. NO CHANGE
- f. Therefore,
- g. However,
- h. Furthermore,

15. Which of the following would be the best choice for this sentence (reproduced below)?

> (11) <u>In May 2015, the United States Bureau of Labor Statistics (BLS) reported that the median annual salary of aircraft engineers was $107,830.</u>

- a. NO CHANGE
- b. May of 2015, the United States Bureau of Labor Statistics (BLS) reported that the median annual salary of aircraft engineers was $107,830.
- c. In May of 2015 the United States Bureau of Labor Statistics (BLS) reported that the median annual salary of aircraft engineers was $107,830.
- d. In May, 2015, the United States Bureau of Labor Statistics (BLS) reported that the median annual salary of aircraft engineers was $107,830.

16. Which of the following would be the best choice for this sentence (reproduced below)?

> (12) <u>Conversely,</u> employment opportunities for aircraft engineers are projected to decrease by 2 percent by 2024.

- e. NO CHANGE
- f. Similarly,
- g. In other words,
- h. Accordingly,

17. Which of the following would be the best choice for this sentence (reproduced below)?

> Conversely, (13) <u>employment opportunities for aircraft engineers are projected to decrease by 2 percent by 2024.</u>

- a. NO CHANGE
- b. employment opportunities for aircraft engineers will be projected to decrease by 2 percent by 2024.
- c. employment opportunities for aircraft engineers is projected to decrease by 2 percent by 2024.
- d. employment opportunities for aircraft engineers was projected to decrease by 2 percent by 2024.

18. Which of the following would be the best choice for this sentence (reproduced below)?

> (14) <u>Nevertheless aircraft engineers who know how to utilize</u> modeling and simulation programs, fluid dynamic software, and robotic engineering tools is projected to remain the most employable.

- e. NO CHANGE
- f. Nevertheless; aircraft engineers who know how to utilize
- g. Nevertheless, aircraft engineers who know how to utilize
- h. Nevertheless—aircraft engineers who know how to utilize

19. Which of the following would be the best choice for this sentence (reproduced below)?

> Nevertheless aircraft engineers who know how to utilize modeling and simulation programs, fluid dynamic software, and robotic engineering tools (15) <u>is projected to remain</u> the most employable.

- a. NO CHANGE
- b. am projected to remain
- c. was projected to remain
- d. are projected to remain

Questions 20–25 are based on the following passage:

> On September 11th, 2001, a group of terrorists hijacked four American airplanes. The terrorists crashed the planes into the World Trade Center in New York City, the Pentagon in Washington D.C., and a field in Pennsylvania. Nearly 3,000 people died during the attacks, which propelled the United States into a (16) <u>"War on Terror".</u>

113

About the Terrorists

(17) <u>Terrorists commonly uses fear and violence to achieve political goals</u>. The nineteen terrorists who orchestrated and implemented the attacks of September 11th were militants associated with al-Qaeda, an Islamic extremist group founded by Osama bin Laden, Abdullah Azzam, and others in the late 1980s. (18) <u>Bin Laden orchestrated the attacks as a response to what he felt was American injustice against Islam and hatred towards Muslims.</u> In his words, "Terrorism against America deserves to be praised."

Islam is the religion of Muslims, (19) <u>who live mainly in south and southwest Asia</u> and Sub-Saharan Africa. The majority of Muslims practice Islam peacefully. However, fractures in Islam have led to the growth of Islamic extremists who strictly oppose Western influences. They seek to institute stringent Islamic law and destroy those who violate Islamic code.

In November 2002, bin Laden provided the explicit motives for the 9/11 terror attacks. According to this list, (20) <u>Americas support of Israel,</u> military presence in Saudi Arabia, and other anti-Muslim actions were the causes.

The Timeline of the Attacks

The morning of September 11 began like any other for most Americans. Then, at 8:45 a.m., a Boeing 767 plane (21) <u>crashed into the north tower of the World Trade Center</u> in New York City. Hundreds were instantly killed. Others were trapped on higher floors. The crash was initially thought to be a freak accident. When a second plane flew directly into the south tower eighteen minutes later, it was determined that America was under attack.

At 9:45 a.m., (22) <u>slamming into the Pentagon was a third plane,</u> America's military headquarters in Washington D.C. The jet fuel of this plane caused a major fire and partial building collapse that resulted in nearly 200 deaths. By 10:00 a.m., the south tower of the World Trade Center collapsed. Thirty minutes later, the north tower followed suit.

While this was happening, a fourth plane that departed from New Jersey, United Flight 93, was hijacked. The passengers learned of the attacks that occurred in New York and Washington D.C. and realized that they faced the same fate as the other planes that crashed. The passengers were determined to overpower the terrorists in an effort to prevent the deaths of additional innocent American citizens. Although the passengers were successful in (23) <u>diverging</u> the plane, it crashed in a western Pennsylvania field and killed everyone on board. The plane's final target remains uncertain, (24) <u>but believed by many people was the fact that United Flight 93 was heading for the White House.</u>

Heroes and Rescuers

(25) <u>Close to 3,000 people died in the World Trade Center attacks.</u> This figure includes 343 New York City firefighters and paramedics, 23 New York City police officers, and 37 Port Authority officers. Nevertheless, thousands of men and women in service worked

114

(26) <u>valiantly</u> to evacuate the buildings, save trapped workers, extinguish infernos, uncover victims trapped in fallen rubble, and tend to nearly 10,000 injured individuals.

About 300 rescue dogs played a major role in the after-attack salvages. Working twelve-hour shifts, the dogs scoured the rubble and alerted paramedics when they found signs of life. While doing so, the dogs served as a source of comfort and therapy for the rescue teams.

Initial Impacts on America

The attacks of September 11, 2001 resulted in the immediate suspension of all air travel. No flights could take off from or land on American soil. (27) <u>American airports and airspace closed to all national and international flights.</u> Therefore, over five hundred flights had to turn back or be redirected to other countries. Canada alone received 226 flights and thousands of stranded passengers. (28) <u>Needless to say, as cancelled flights are rescheduled, air travel became backed up and chaotic for quite some time.</u>

At the time of the attacks, George W. Bush was the president of the United States. President Bush announced that "We will make no distinction between the terrorists who committed these acts and those who harbor them." The rate of hate crimes against American Muslims spiked, despite President Bush's call for the country to treat them with respect.

Additionally, relief funds were quickly arranged. The funds were used to support families of the victims, orphaned children, and those with major injuries. In this way, the tragic event brought the citizens together through acts of service towards those directly impacted by the attack.

Long-Term Effects of the Attacks

Over the past fifteen years, the attacks of September 11th have transformed the United States' government, travel safety protocols, and international relations. Anti-terrorism legislation became a priority for many countries as law enforcement and intelligence agencies teamed up to find and defeat alleged terrorists.

Present George W. Bush announced a War on Terror. He (29) <u>desired</u> to bring bin Laden and al-Qaeda to justice and prevent future terrorist networks from gaining strength. The War in Afghanistan began in October of 2001 when the United States and British forces bombed al-Qaeda camps. (30) <u>The Taliban, a group of fundamentalist Muslims who protected Osama bin Laden, was overthrown on December 9, 2001. However, the war continued in order to defeat insurgency campaigns in neighboring countries.</u> Ten years later, the United State Navy SEALS killed Osama bin Laden in Pakistan. During 2014, the United States declared the end of its involvement in the War on Terror in Afghanistan.

Museums and memorials have since been erected to honor and remember the thousands of people who died during the September 11th attacks, including the brave rescue workers who gave their lives in the effort to help others.

20. Which of the following would be the best choice for this sentence (reproduced below)?

> Nearly 3,000 people died during the attacks, which propelled the United States into a (16) <u>"War on Terror"</u>.

   e. NO CHANGE
   f. "war on terror".
   g. "war on terror."
   h. "War on Terror."

21. Which of the following would be the best choice for this sentence (reproduced below)?

> (17) <u>Terrorists commonly uses fear and violence to achieve political goals.</u>

   a. NO CHANGE
   b. Terrorist's commonly use fear and violence to achieve political goals.
   c. Terrorists commonly use fear and violence to achieve political goals.
   d. Terrorists commonly use fear and violence to achieves political goals.

22. Which of the following would be the best choice for this sentence (reproduced below)?

> (18) <u>Bin Laden orchestrated the attacks as a response to what he felt was American injustice against Islam and hatred towards Muslims.</u>

   e. NO CHANGE
   f. Bin Laden orchestrated the attacks as a response to what he felt was American injustice against Islam, and hatred towards Muslims.
   g. Bin Laden orchestrated the attacks, as a response to what he felt was American injustice against Islam and hatred towards Muslims.
   h. Bin Laden orchestrated the attacks as responding to what he felt was American injustice against Islam and hatred towards Muslims.

23. Which of the following would be the best choice for this sentence (reproduced below)?

> Islam is the religion of Muslims, (19) <u>who live mainly in south and southwest Asia</u> and Sub-Saharan Africa.

   a. NO CHANGE
   b. who live mainly in South and Southwest Asia
   c. who live mainly in the south and Southwest Asia
   d. who live mainly in the south and southwest asia

24. Which of the following would be the best choice for this sentence (reproduced below)?

> According to this list, (20) <u>Americas support of Israel,</u> military presence in Saudi Arabia, and other anti-Muslim actions were the causes.

   e. NO CHANGE
   f. America's support of israel,
   g. Americas support of Israel
   h. America's support of Israel,

25. Which of the following would be the best choice for this sentence (reproduced below)?

> Then, at 8:45 a.m., a Boeing 767 plane (21) <u>crashed into the north tower of the World Trade Center</u> in New York City.

   a. NO CHANGE
   b. crashes into the north tower of the World Trade Center
   c. crashing into the north tower of the World Trade Center
   d. crash into the north tower of the World Trade Center

Reading Comprehension

Read the following poem and answer questions 26 & 27.

> Two roads diverged in a yellow wood,
> And sorry I could not travel both
> And be one traveler, long I stood
> And looked down one as far as I could
> To where it bent in the undergrowth;   *5*
>
> Then took the other, as just as fair,
> And having perhaps the better claim,
> Because it was grassy and wanted wear;
> Though as for that the passing there
> Had worn them really about the same,   *10*
>
> And both that morning equally lay
> In leaves no step had trodden black.
> Oh, I kept the first for another day!
> Yet knowing how way leads on to way,
> I doubted if I should ever come back.   *15*
>
> I shall be telling this with a sigh
> Somewhere ages and ages hence:
> Two roads diverged in a wood, and I—
> I took the one less traveled by,
> And that has made all the difference.   *20*

"The Road Not Taken" by Robert Frost

117

26. Which option best expresses the symbolic meaning of the "road" and the overall theme?
    e. A divergent spot where the traveler had to choose the correct path to his destination
    f. A choice between good and evil that the traveler needs to make
    g. The traveler's struggle between his lost love and his future prospects
    h. Life's journey and the choices with which humans are faced

27. Which line best contributes to the idea that the second path was *less traveled*?
    a. 5
    b. 4
    c. 8
    d. 10

Questions 28–33 are based upon the following passage:

"Did you ever come across a protégé of his—one Hyde?" he asked.

"Hyde?" repeated Lanyon. "No. Never heard of him. Since my time."

That was the amount of information that the lawyer carried back with him to the great, dark bed on which he tossed to and fro until the small hours of the morning began to grow large. It was a night of little ease to his toiling mind, toiling in mere darkness and besieged by questions.

Six o'clock struck on the bells of the church that was so conveniently near to Mr. Utterson's dwelling, and still he was digging at the problem. Hitherto it had touched him on the intellectual side alone; but now his imagination also was engaged, or rather enslaved; and as he lay and tossed in the gross darkness of the night in the curtained room, Mr. Enfield's tale went by before his mind in a scroll of lighted pictures. He would be aware of the great field of lamps in a nocturnal city; then of the figure of a man walking swiftly; then of a child running from the doctor's; and then these met, and that human Juggernaut trod the child down and passed on regardless of her screams. Or else he would see a room in a rich house, where his friend lay asleep, dreaming and smiling at his dreams; and then the door of that room would be opened, the curtains of the bed plucked apart, the sleeper recalled, and, lo! There would stand by his side a figure to whom power was given, and even at that dead hour he must rise and do its bidding. The figure in these two phases haunted the lawyer all night; and if at any time he dozed over, it was but to see it glide more stealthily through sleeping houses, or move the more swiftly, and still the more smoothly, even to dizziness, through wider labyrinths of lamplighted city, and at every street corner crush a child and leave her screaming. And still the figure had no face by which he might know it; even in his dreams it had no face, or one that baffled him and melted before his eyes; and thus it was that there sprung up and grew apace in the lawyer's mind a singularly strong, almost an inordinate, curiosity to behold the features of the real Mr. Hyde. If he could but once set eyes on him, he thought the mystery would lighten and perhaps roll altogether away, as was the habit of mysterious things when well examined. He might see a reason for his friend's strange preference or bondage, and even for the startling clauses of the will. And at least it would be a face worth seeing: the face of a man who

118

was without bowels of mercy: a face which had but to show itself to raise up, in the mind of the unimpressionable Enfield, a spirit of enduring hatred.

From that time forward, Mr. Utterson began to haunt the door in the by-street of shops. In the morning before office hours, at noon when business was plenty and time scarce, at night under the face of the fogged city moon, by all lights and at all hours of solitude or concourse, the lawyer was to be found on his chosen post.

"If he be Mr. Hyde," he had thought, "I should be Mr. Seek."

Excerpt from The Strange Case of Dr. Jekyll and Mr. Hyde by Robert Louis Stevenson

28. What is the purpose of the use of repetition in the following passage?
It was a night of little ease to his toiling mind, toiling in mere darkness and besieged by questions.

e. It serves as a demonstration of the mental state of Mr. Lanyon.
f. It is reminiscent of the church bells that are mentioned in the story.
g. It mimics Mr. Utterson's ambivalence.
h. It emphasizes Mr. Utterson's anguish in failing to identify Hyde's whereabouts.

29. What is the setting of the story in this passage?
a. In the city
b. On the countryside
c. In a jail
d. In a mental health facility

30. What can one infer about the meaning of the word *Juggernaut* from the author's use of it in the passage?
e. It is an apparition that appears at daybreak.
f. It scares children.
g. It is associated with space travel.
h. Mr. Utterson finds it soothing.

31. What is the definition of the word *haunt* in the following passage?

From that time forward, Mr. Utterson began to haunt the door in the by-street of shops. In the morning before office hours, at noon when business was plenty and time scarce, at night under the face of the fogged city moon, by all lights and at all hours of solitude or concourse, the lawyer was to be found on his chosen post.

a. To levitate
b. To constantly visit
c. To terrorize
d. To daunt

32. The phrase *labyrinths of lamplighted city* contains an example of what?
    e. Hyperbole
    f. Simile
    g. Juxtaposition
    h. Alliteration

33. What can one reasonably conclude from the final comment of this passage?

    "If he be Mr. Hyde," he had thought, "I should be Mr. Seek."

    a. The speaker is considering a name change.
    b. The speaker is experiencing an identity crisis.
    c. The speaker has mistakenly been looking for the wrong person.
    d. The speaker intends to continue to look for Hyde.

Questions 34–39 are based upon the following passage:

My gentleness and good behaviour had gained so far on the emperor and his court, and indeed upon the army and people in general, that I began to conceive hopes of getting my liberty in a short time. I took all possible methods to cultivate this favourable disposition. The natives came, by degrees, to be less apprehensive of any danger from me. I would sometimes lie down, and let five or six of them dance on my hand; and at last the boys and girls would venture to come and play at hide-and-seek in my hair. I had now made a good progress in understanding and speaking the language. The emperor had a mind one day to entertain me with several of the country shows, wherein they exceed all nations I have known, both for dexterity and magnificence. I was diverted with none so much as that of the rope-dancers, performed upon a slender white thread, extended about two feet, and twelve inches from the ground. Upon which I shall desire liberty, with the reader's patience, to enlarge a little.

This diversion is only practised by those persons who are candidates for great employments, and high favour at court. They are trained in this art from their youth, and are not always of noble birth, or liberal education. When a great office is vacant, either by death or disgrace (which often happens), five or six of those candidates petition the emperor to entertain his majesty and the court with a dance on the rope; and whoever jumps the highest, without falling, succeeds in the office. Very often the chief ministers themselves are commanded to show their skill, and to convince the emperor that they have not lost their faculty. Flimnap, the treasurer, is allowed to cut a caper on the straight rope, at least an inch higher than any other lord in the whole empire. I have seen him do the summerset several times together, upon a trencher fixed on a rope which is no thicker than a common packthread in England. My friend Reldresal, principal secretary for private affairs, is, in my opinion, if I am not partial, the second after the treasurer; the rest of the great officers are much upon a par.

Excerpt from Gulliver's Travels into Several Remote Nations of the World by Jonathan Swift

120

34. Which of the following statements best summarizes the central purpose of this text?
    e. Gulliver details his fondness for the archaic yet interesting practices of his captors.
    f. Gulliver conjectures about the intentions of the aristocratic sector of society.
    g. Gulliver becomes acquainted with the people and practices of his new surroundings.
    h. Gulliver's differences cause him to become penitent around new acquaintances.

35. What is the word *principal* referring to in the following text?

    My friend Reldresal, principal secretary for private affairs, is, in my opinion, if I am not partial, the second after the treasurer; the rest of the great officers are much upon a par.

    a. Primary or chief
    b. An acolyte
    c. An individual who provides nurturing
    d. One in a subordinate position

36. What can the reader infer from the following text?

    I would sometimes lie down, and let five or six of them dance on my hand; and at last the boys and girls would venture to come and play at hide-and-seek in my hair.

    e. The children tortured Gulliver.
    f. Gulliver traveled because he wanted to meet new people.
    g. Gulliver is considerably larger than the children who are playing around him.
    h. Gulliver has a genuine love and enthusiasm for people of all sizes.

37. What is the significance of the word *mind* in the following passage?

    The emperor had a mind one day to entertain me with several of the country shows, wherein they exceed all nations I have known, both for dexterity and magnificence.

    a. The ability to think
    b. A collective vote
    c. A definitive decision
    d. A mythological question

38. Which of the following assertions does NOT support the fact that games are a commonplace event in this culture?
    e. My gentleness and good behavior ... short time.
    f. They are trained in this art from their youth ... liberal education.
    g. Very often the chief ministers themselves are commanded to show their skill ... not lost their faculty.
    h. Flimnap, the treasurer, is allowed to cut a caper on the straight rope ... higher than any other lord in the whole empire.

39. How do Flimnap and Reldresal demonstrate the community's emphasis on physical strength and leadership abilities?
    a. Only children used Gulliver's hands as a playground.
    b. The two men who exhibited superior abilities held prominent positions in the community.
    c. Only common townspeople, not leaders, walk the straight rope.
    d. No one could jump higher than Gulliver.

Questions 40–45 are based upon the following passage:

> Four score and seven years ago our fathers brought forth on this continent, a new nation, conceived in Liberty, and dedicated to the proposition that all men are created equal.
>
> Now we are engaged in a great civil war, testing whether that nation, or any nation so conceived and so dedicated, can long endure. We are met on a great battle-field of that war. We have come to dedicate a portion of that field, as a final resting place for those who here gave their lives that that nation might live. It is altogether fitting and proper that we should do this.
>
> But, in a larger sense, we can not dedicate—we can not consecrate—we can not hallow—this ground. The brave men, living and dead, who struggled here, have consecrated it, far above our poor power to add or detract. The world will little note, nor long remember what we say here, but it can never forget what they did here. It is for us the living, rather, to be dedicated here to the unfinished work which they who fought here have thus far so nobly advanced. It is rather for us to be here dedicated to the great task remaining before us—that from these honored dead we take increased devotion to that cause for which they gave the last full measure of devotion—that we here highly resolve that these dead shall not have died in vain—that this nation, under God, shall have a new birth of freedom—and that government of the people, by the people, for the people, shall not perish from the earth.

Abraham Lincoln's Address Delivered at the Dedication of the Cemetery at Gettysburg, November 19, 1863

40. The best description for the phrase *four score and seven years ago* is which of the following?
    e. A unit of measurement
    f. A period of time
    g. A literary movement
    h. A statement of political reform

41. What is the setting of this text?
    a. A battleship off of the coast of France
    b. A desert plain on the Sahara Desert
    c. A battlefield in North America
    d. The residence of Abraham Lincoln

122

42. Which war is Abraham Lincoln referring to in the following passage?

> Now we are engaged in a great civil war, testing whether that nation, or any nation so conceived and so dedicated, can long endure.

    e. World War I
    f. The War of the Spanish Succession
    g. World War II
    h. The American Civil War

43. What message is the author trying to convey through this address?
    a. The audience should perpetuate the ideals of freedom that the soldiers died fighting for.
    b. The audience should honor the dead by establishing an annual memorial service.
    c. The audience should form a militia that would overturn the current political structure.
    d. The audience should forget the lives that were lost and discredit the soldiers.

44. Which rhetorical device is being used in the following passage?

> ...we here highly resolve that these dead shall not have died in vain—that this nation, under God, shall have a new birth of freedom—and that government of the people, by the people, for the people, shall not perish from the earth.

    e. Antimetabole
    f. Antiphrasis
    g. Anaphora
    h. Epiphora

45. What is the effect of Lincoln's statement in the following passage?

> But, in a larger sense, we can not dedicate—we can not consecrate—we can not hallow—this ground. The brave men, living and dead, who struggled here, have consecrated it, far above our poor power to add or detract.

    a. His comparison emphasizes the great sacrifice of the soldiers who fought in the war.
    b. His comparison serves as a remainder of the inadequacies of his audience.
    c. His comparison serves as a catalyst for guilt and shame among audience members.
    d. His comparison attempts to illuminate the great differences between soldiers and civilians.

Questions 46–50 are based on the following passage:

> MANKIND being originally equals in the order of creation, the equality could only be destroyed by some subsequent circumstance; the distinctions of rich, and poor, may in a great measure be accounted for, Oppression is often the CONSEQUENCE , but seldom or never the MEANS of riches; Oppression is often the consequence, but seldom or never the means of riches; and though avarice will preserve a man from being necessitously poor, it generally makes him too timorous to be wealthy.
>
> But there is another and greater distinction for which no truly natural or religious reason can be assigned, and that is, the distinction of men into KINGS and SUBJECTS. Male and female are the distinctions of nature, good and bad the distinctions of heaven; but how

123

a race of men came into the world so exalted above the rest, and distinguished like some new species, is worth enquiring into, and whether they are the means of happiness or of misery to mankind.

In the early ages of the world, according to the scripture chronology, there were no kings; the consequence of which was there were no wars; it is the pride of kings which throw mankind into confusion. Holland without a king hath enjoyed more peace for this last century than any of the monarchical governments in Europe. Antiquity favors the same remark; for the quiet and rural lives of the first patriarchs hath a happy something in them, which vanishes away when we come to the history of Jewish royalty.

Government by kings was first introduced into the world by the Heathens, from whom the children of Israel copied the custom. It was the most prosperous invention the Devil ever set on foot for the promotion of idolatry. The Heathens paid divine honors to their deceased kings, and the Christian world hath improved on the plan, by doing the same to their living ones. How impious is the title of sacred majesty applied to a worm, who in the midst of his splendor is crumbling into dust!

As the exalting one man so greatly above the rest cannot be justified on the equal rights of nature, so neither can it be defended on the authority of scripture; for the will of the Almighty, as declared by Gideon and the prophet Samuel, expressly disapproves of government by kings. All anti-monarchical parts of scripture have been very smoothly glossed over in monarchical governments, but they undoubtedly merit the attention of countries which have their governments yet to form. RENDER UNTO CAESAR THE THINGS WHICH ARE CAESAR'S is the scripture doctrine of courts, yet it is no support of monarchical government, for the Jews at that time were without a king, and in a state of vassalage to the Romans.

Now three thousand years passed away from the Mosaic account of the creation, till the Jews under a national delusion requested a king. Till then their form of government (except in extraordinary cases, where the Almighty interposed) was a kind of republic administered by a judge and the elders of the tribes. Kings they had none, and it was held sinful to acknowledge any being under that title but the Lord of Hosts. And when a man seriously reflects on the idolatrous homage which is paid to the persons of kings, he need not wonder that the Almighty, ever jealous of his honor, should disapprove of a form of government which so impiously invades the prerogative of heaven.

Excerpt From "Common Sense" by Thomas Paine

46. According to the passage, what role does avarice, or greed, play in poverty?
   e. Avarice makes a man poor.
   f. Avarice is the consequence of wealth.
   g. Avarice prevents a man from being poor, but makes him too fearful to be wealthy.
   h. Avarice is what drives a person to be very wealthy

47. Of these distinctions, which does the author believe to be beyond natural or religious reason?
    a. Good and bad
    b. Male and female
    c. Human and animal
    d. King and subjects

48. According to the passage, what are the Heathens responsible for?
    e. Government by kings
    f. Quiet and rural lives of patriarchs
    g. Paying divine honors to their living kings
    h. Equal rights of nature

49. Which of the following best states Paine's rationale for the denouncement of monarchy?
    a. It is against the laws of nature
    b. It is against the equal rights of nature and is denounced in scripture
    c. Despite scripture, a monarchal government is unlawful
    d. Neither the law nor scripture denounce monarchy

50. Based on the passage, what is the best definition of the word *idolatrous*?
    e. Worshipping heroes
    f. Being deceitful
    g. Sinfulness
    h. Engaging in illegal activities

Questions 51–56 are based upon the following passage:

Fellow-citizens, pardon me, allow me to ask, why am I called upon to speak here to-day? What have I, or those I represent, to do with your national independence? Are the great principles of political freedom and of natural justice, embodied in that Declaration of Independence, extended to us? And am I, therefore, called upon to bring our humble offering to the national altar, and to confess the benefits and express devout gratitude for the blessings resulting from your independence to us?

Would to God, both for your sakes and ours, that an affirmative answer could be truthfully returned to these questions! Then would my task be light, and my burden easy and delightful. For who is there so cold, that a nation's sympathy could not warm him? Who so obdurate and dead to the claims of gratitude, that would not thankfully acknowledge such priceless benefits? Who so stolid and selfish, that would not give his voice to swell the hallelujahs of a nation's jubilee, when the chains of servitude had been torn from his limbs? I am not that man. In a case like that, the dumb my eloquently speak, and the lame man leap as an hart.

But, such is not the state of the case. I say it with a sad sense of the disparity between us. I am not included within the pale of this glorious and anniversary! Your high independence only reveals the immeasurable distance between us. The blessings in which you, this day, rejoice, are not enjoyed in common. The rich inheritance of justice, liberty, prosperity and independence, bequeathed by your fathers, is shared by *you*, not by *me*. The sunlight that brought life and healing to *you*, has brought stripes and death

125

to *me*. This Fourth [of] July is *yours*, not *mine*. *You* may rejoice, *I* must mourn. To drag a man in fetters into the grand illuminated temple of liberty, and call upon him to join you in joyous anthems, were inhuman mockery and sacrilegious irony. Do you mean, citizens, to mock me, by asking me to speak to-day? If so, there is a parallel to your conduct. And let me warn you that it is dangerous to copy the example of a nation whose crimes, lowering up to heaven, were thrown down by the breath of the Almighty, burying that nation in irrecoverable ruin! I can to-day take up the plaintive lament of a peeled and woe-smitten people!

"By the rivers of Babylon, there we sat down. Yea! we wept when we remembered Zion. We hanged our harps upon the willows in the midst thereof. For there, they that carried us away captive, required of us a song; and they who wasted us required of us mirth, saying, 'Sing us one of the songs of Zion.' How can we sing the Lord's song in a strange land? If I forget thee, O Jerusalem, let my right hand forget her cunning. If I do not remember thee, let my tongue cleave to the roof of my mouth."

Excerpt from "What to the Slave is the Fourth of July?" by Frederick Douglass, Rochester, New York
July 5, 1852

51. What is the tone of the first paragraph of this passage?
   a. Incredulous
   b. Inclusive
   c. Contemplative
   d. Nonchalant

52. Which word CANNOT be used synonymously with the term *obdurate* as it is conveyed in the text below?

   Who so obdurate and dead to the claims of gratitude, that would not thankfully acknowledge such priceless benefits?

   e. Steadfast
   f. Stubborn
   g. Contented
   h. Unwavering

53. What is the central purpose of this text?
   a. To demonstrate the author's extensive knowledge of the Bible
   b. To address the hypocrisy of the Fourth of July holiday
   c. To convince wealthy landowners to adopt new holiday rituals
   d. To explain why minorities often relished the notion of segregation in government institutions

54. Which statement serves as evidence for question 53 above?
   e. By the rivers of Babylon, there we sat down.
   f. Fellow-citizens, pardon me, allow me to ask, why am I called upon to speak here to-day?
   g. I can to-day take up the plaintive lament of a peeled and woe-smitten people!
   h. The rich inheritance of justice, liberty, prosperity and independence, bequeathed by your fathers, is shared by you, not by me.

55. The statement below features an example of which of the following literary devices?

Your high independence only reveals the immeasurable distance between us.

a. Assonance
b. Parallelism
c. Amplification
d. Hyperbole

56. The speaker's use of biblical references, such as "rivers of Babylon" and the "songs of Zion," helps the reader to do all EXCEPT which of the following?

e. Identify with the speaker using common text
f. Draw a connection between another group of people who have been affected by slavery and American slaves
g. Recognize the equivocation of the speaker and those that he represents
h. Appeal to the listener's sense of humanity

Questions 57–62 are based upon the following passage:

Three years ago, I think there were not many bird-lovers in the United States who believed it possible to prevent the total extinction of both egrets from our fauna. All the known rookeries accessible to plume-hunters had been totally destroyed. Two years ago, the secret discovery of several small, hidden colonies prompted William Dutcher, President of the National Association of Audubon Societies, and Mr. T. Gilbert Pearson, Secretary, to attempt the protection of those colonies. With a fund contributed for the purpose, wardens were hired and duly commissioned. As previously stated, one of those wardens was shot dead in cold blood by a plume hunter. The task of guarding swamp rookeries from the attacks of money-hungry desperadoes, to whom the accursed plumes were worth their weight in gold, is a very chancy proceeding. There is now one warden in Florida who says that "before they get my rookery they will first have to get me."

Thus far the protective work of the Audubon Association has been successful. Now there are twenty colonies, which contain all told, about 5,000 egrets and about 120,000 herons and ibises which are guarded by the Audubon wardens. One of the most important is on Bird Island, a mile out in Orange Lake, central Florida, and it is ably defended by Oscar E. Baynard. To-day, the plume hunters who do not dare to raid the guarded rookeries are trying to study out the lines of flight of the birds, to and from their feeding-grounds, and shoot them in transit. Their motto is—"Anything to beat the law, and get the plumes." It is there that the state of Florida should take part in the war.

The success of this campaign is attested by the fact that last year a number of egrets were seen in eastern Massachusetts—for the first time in many years. And so to-day the question is, can the wardens continue to hold the plume-hunters at bay?

Excerpt from *Our Vanishing Wildlife* by William T. Hornaday

127

57. The author's use of first-person pronouns in the following text does NOT have which of the following effects?

> Three years ago, I think there were not many bird-lovers in the United States who believed it possible to prevent the total extinction of both egrets from our fauna.

 a. The phrase "I think" acts as a sort of hedging, where the author's tone is less direct and/or absolute.

 b. It allows the reader to more easily connect with the author.

 c. It encourages the reader to empathize with the egrets.

 d. It distances the reader from the text by overemphasizing the story.

58. What purpose does the quote serve at the end of the first paragraph?

 e. The quote shows proof of a hunter threatening one of the wardens.

 f. The quote lightens the mood by illustrating the colloquial language of the region.

 g. The quote provides an example of a warden protecting one of the colonies.

 h. The quote provides much needed comic relief in the form of a joke.

59. What is the meaning of the word *rookeries* in the following text?

> To-day, the plume hunters who do not dare to raid the guarded rookeries are trying to study out the lines of flight of the birds, to and from their feeding-grounds, and shoot them in transit.

 a. Houses in a slum area

 b. A place where hunters gather to trade tools

 c. A place where wardens go to trade stories

 d. A colony of breeding birds

60. What is on Bird Island?

 e. Hunters selling plumes

 f. An important bird colony

 g. Bird Island Battle between the hunters and the wardens

 h. An important egret with unique plumes

61. What is the main purpose of the passage?

 a. To persuade the audience to act in preservation of the bird colonies

 b. To show the effect hunting egrets has had on the environment

 c. To argue that the preservation of bird colonies has had a negative impact on the environment

 d. To demonstrate the success of the protective work of the Audubon Association

62. Why are hunters trying to study the lines of flight of the birds?

 e. To study ornithology, which requires knowing the lines of flight that birds take.

 f. To help wardens preserve the lives of the birds

 g. To have a better opportunity to hunt the birds

 h. To build their homes under the lines of flight because they believe it brings good luck

Questions 63–67 are based upon the following passage:

Insects as a whole are preeminently creatures of the land and the air. This is shown not only by the possession of wings by a vast majority of the class, but by the mode of breathing to which reference has already been made, a system of branching air-tubes carrying atmospheric air with its combustion-supporting oxygen to all the insect's tissues. The air gains access to these tubes through a number of paired air-holes or spiracles, arranged segmentally in series.

It is of great interest to find that, nevertheless, a number of insects spend much of their time under water. This is true of not a few in the perfect winged state, as for example aquatic beetles and water-bugs ('boatmen' and 'scorpions') which have some way of protecting their spiracles when submerged, and, possessing usually the power of flight, can pass on occasion from pond or stream to upper air. But it is advisable in connection with our present subject to dwell especially on some insects that remain continually under water till they are ready to undergo their final moult and attain the winged state, which they pass entirely in the air. The preparatory instars of such insects are aquatic; the adult instar is aerial. All may-flies, dragon-flies, and caddis-flies, many beetles and two-winged flies, and a few moths thus divide their life-story between the water and the air. For the present we confine attention to the Stone-flies, the May-flies, and the Dragon-flies, three well-known orders of insects respectively called by systematists the Plecoptera, the Ephemeroptera, and the Odonata.

In the case of many insects that have aquatic larvae, the latter are provided with some arrangement for enabling them to reach atmospheric air through the surface-film of the water. But the larva of a stone-fly, a dragon-fly, or a may-fly is adapted more completely than these for aquatic life; it can, by means of gills of some kind, breathe the air dissolved in water.

Excerpt from The Life-Story of Insects by Geo H. Carpenter

63. Which statement best details the central idea in this passage?
  a. It introduces certain insects that transition from water to air.
  b. It delves into entomology, especially where gills are concerned.
  c. It defines what constitutes insects' breathing.
  d. It invites readers to have a hand in the preservation of insects.

64. Which definition most closely relates to the usage of the word *moult* in the passage?
  e. An adventure of sorts, especially underwater
  f. Mating act between two insects
  g. The act of shedding part or all of the outer shell
  h. Death of an organism that ends in a revival of life

65. What is the purpose of the first paragraph in relation to the second paragraph?
  a. The first paragraph serves as a cause, and the second paragraph serves as an effect.
  b. The first paragraph serves as a contrast to the second.
  c. The first paragraph is a description for the argument in the second paragraph.
  d. The first and second paragraphs are merely presented in a sequence.

129

66. What does the following sentence most nearly mean?

> The preparatory instars of such insects are aquatic; the adult instar is aerial.

e. The volume of water is necessary to prep the insect for transition rather than the volume of the air.
f. The abdomen of the insect is designed like a star in the water as well as the air.
g. The stage of preparation in between molting is acted out in the water, while the last stage is in the air.
h. These insects breathe first in the water through gills, yet continue to use the same organs to breathe in the air.

67. Which of the statements reflect information that one could reasonably infer based on the author's tone?
a. The author's tone is persuasive and attempts to call the audience to action.
b. The author's tone is passionate due to excitement over the subject and personal narrative.
c. The author's tone is informative and exhibits interest in the subject of the study.
d. The author's tone is somber, depicting some anger at the state of insect larvae.

Math

1. If $6t + 4 = 16$, what is t?
a. 1
b. 2
c. 3
d. 4

2. The variable y is directly proportional to x. If $y = 3$ when $x = 5$, then what is y when $x = 20$?
e. 10
f. 12
g. 14
h. 16

3. A line passes through the point $(1, 2)$ and crosses the y-axis at $y = 1$. Which of the following is an equation for this line?
a. $y = 2x$
b. $y = x + 1$
c. $x + y = 1$
d. $y = \frac{x}{2} - 2$

4. There are $4x + 1$ treats in each party favor bag. If a total of $60x + 15$ treats are distributed, how many bags are given out?
e. 15
f. 16
g. 20
h. 22

5. An accounting firm charted its income on the following pie graph. If the total income for the year was $500,000, how much of the income was received from Audit and Taxation Services?

Income

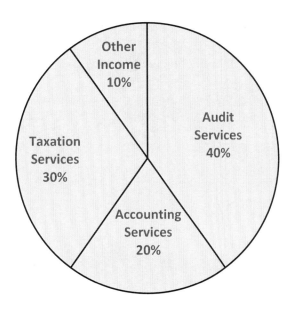

a. $200,000
b. $350,000
c. $150,000
d. $300,000

6. What are the roots of $x^2 + x - 2$?
    e. 1 and -2
    f. -1 and 2
    g. 2 and -2
    h. 9 and 13

7. What is the y-intercept of $y = x^{5/3} + (x - 3)(x + 1)$?
    a. 3.5
    b. 7.6
    c. -3
    d. -15.1

8. The phone bill is calculated each month using the equation $c = 50g + 75$. The cost of the phone bill per month is represented by c, and g represents the gigabytes of data used that month. What is the value and interpretation of the slope of this equation?

    e. 75 dollars per day

    f. 75 gigabytes per day

    g. 50 dollars per day

    h. 50 dollars per gigabyte

9. $(4x^2y^4)^{\frac{3}{2}}$ can be simplified to which of the following?

    a. $8x^3y^6$

    b. $4x^{\frac{5}{2}}y$

    c. $4xy$

    d. $32x^{\frac{7}{2}}y^{\frac{11}{2}}$

10. If $\sqrt{1 + x} = 4$, what is x?

    e. 10

    f. 15

    g. 20

    h. 25

11. Suppose $\frac{x+2}{x} = 2$. What is x?

    a. -1

    b. 0

    c. 2

    d. 4

12. Which graph will be a line parallel to the graph of $y = 3x - 2$?

    e. $6x - 2y = -2$

    f. $4x - y = -4$

    g. $3y = x - 2$

    h. $2x - 2y = 2$

13. A rectangle has a length that is 5 feet longer than three times its width. If the perimeter is 90 feet, what is the length in feet?

    a. 10

    b. 20

    c. 25

    d. 35

14. Five students take a test. The scores of the first four students are 80, 85, 75, and 60. If the median score is 80, which of the following could NOT be the score of the fifth student?

    e. 60

    f. 80

    g. 85

    h. 100

15. In an office, there are 50 workers. A total of 60% of the workers are women, and 50% of the women are wearing skirts. If no men are wearing skirts, how many workers are wearing skirts?
   a. 12
   b. 15
   c. 16
   d. 20

16. Ten students take a test. Five students get a 50. Four students get a 70. If the average score is 55, what was the last student's score?
   e. 20
   f. 40
   g. 50
   h. 60

17. A company invests $50,000 in a building where they can produce saws. If the cost of producing one saw is $40, then which function expresses the amount of money the company pays? The variable y is the money paid and x is the number of saws produced.
   a. $y = 50,000x + 40$
   b. $y + 40 = x - 50,000$
   c. $y = 40x - 50,000$
   d. $y = 40x + 50,000$

18. A six-sided die is rolled. What is the probability that the roll is 1 or 2?
   e. $\frac{1}{6}$
   f. $\frac{1}{4}$
   g. $\frac{1}{3}$
   h. $\frac{1}{2}$

19. A line passes through the origin and through the point $(-3, 4)$. What is the slope of the line?
   a. $-\frac{4}{3}$
   b. $-\frac{3}{4}$
   c. $\frac{4}{3}$
   d. $\frac{3}{4}$

20. An equilateral triangle has a perimeter of 18 feet. The sides of a square have the same length as the triangle's sides. What is the area of the square?
   e. 6 square feet
   f. 36 square feet
   g. 256 square feet
   h. 1,000 square feet

133

21. Change $3\frac{3}{5}$ to a decimal.
    a. 3.6
    b. 4.67
    c. 5.3
    d. 0.28

22. The chart below shows the average car sales for the months of July through December for two different car dealers. What is the average number of cars sold per month in the given time period for Dealer 1?

    e. 7
    f. 11
    g. 9
    h. 8

23. The soccer team is selling donuts to raise money to buy new uniforms. For every box of donuts they sell, the team receives $3 towards their new uniforms. There are 15 people on the team. How many boxes does each player need to sell in order to raise a total of $270 for their new uniforms?
    a. 6
    b. 30
    c. 18
    d. 5

24. What is the value of x in the diagram below?

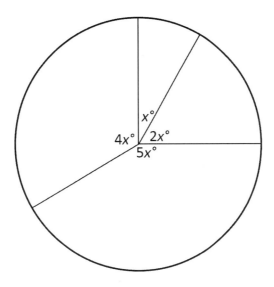

    e. 60
    f. 50
    g. 30
    h. 36

25. What is the probability of randomly picking the winner and runner-up from a race of four horses and distinguishing which is the winner?

    a. $\frac{1}{4}$

    b. $\frac{1}{2}$

    c. $\frac{1}{16}$

    d. $\frac{1}{12}$

26. A figure skater is facing north when she begins to spin to her right. She spins 2,250 degrees. Which direction is she facing when she finishes her spin?

    e. North
    f. South
    g. East
    h. West

27. What is the measure of angle P?

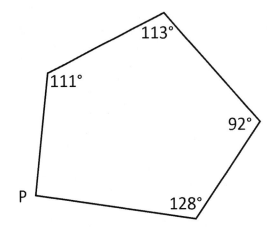

a. 84 degrees
b. 92 degrees
c. 96 degrees
d. 113 degrees

28. The expression $\frac{x-4}{x^2-6x+8}$ is undefined for what value(s) of x?

e. 4 and 2
f. -4 and -2
g. 2
h. 4

29. Nina has a jar where she puts her loose change at the end of each day. There are 13 quarters, 25 dimes, 18 nickels, and 30 pennies in the jar. If she chooses a coin at random, what is the probability that the coin will NOT be a penny or a dime?

a. 0.36
b. 0.64
c. 0.56
d. 0.34

30. The Cross family is planning a trip to Florida. They will be taking two cars for the trip. One car gets 18 miles to the gallon of gas. The other car gets 25 miles to the gallon. If the total trip to Florida is 450 miles, and the cost of gas is $2.49/gallon, how much will the gas cost for both cars to complete the trip?

e. $43.00
f. $44.82
g. $107.07
h. $32.33

31. Add and express in reduced form $\frac{14}{33} + \frac{10}{11}$.

   a. $\frac{2}{11}$

   b. $\frac{6}{11}$

   c. $\frac{4}{3}$

   d. $\frac{44}{33}$

32. 32 is 25% of what number?

   e. 64
   f. 128
   g. 12.65
   h. 8

33. If $3x - 4 + 5x = 8 - 10x$, what is the value of x?

   a. 6
   b. -6
   c. 0.5
   d. 0.67

34. Given the triangle below, find the value of x if $y = 21$.

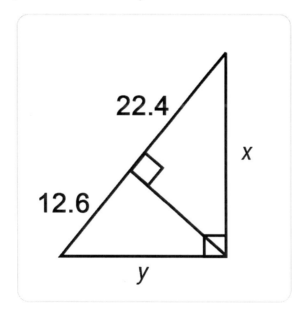

   e. 35
   f. 28
   g. 25
   h. 26

35. Of the given sets of coordinates below, which one lies on the line that is perpendicular to $y = 2x - 3$ and passes through the point $(0, 5)$?
    a. $(2, 4)$
    b. $(-2, 7)$
    c. $(4, -3)$
    d. $(-6, 10)$

36. Which of the following is a factor of both $x^2 + 4x + 4$ and $x^2 - x - 6$?
    e. $x - 3$
    f. $x + 2$
    g. $x - 2$
    h. $x + 3$

37. If $g(x) = x^3 - 3x^2 - 2x + 6$ and $f(x) = 2$, then what is $g(f(x))$?
    a. -26
    b. 6
    c. $2x^3 - 6x^2 - 4x + 12$
    d. -2

38. Which of the following is an equivalent measurement for 1.3 cm?
    e. 0.13 m
    f. 0.013 m
    g. 0.13 mm
    h. 0.013 mm

39. Divide $1,015 \div 1.4$.
    a. 7,250
    b. 725
    c. 7.25
    d. 72.50

40. What is the solution to the following system of equations?

$$x^2 - 2x + y = 8$$

$$x - y = -2$$

    e. $(-2, 3)$
    f. There is no solution.
    g. $(-2, 0) (1, 3)$
    h. $(-2, 0) (3, 5)$

41. What is the simplified form of the expression $(7n + 3n^3 + 3) + (8n + 5n^3 + 2n^4)$?
    a. $9n^4 + 15n - 2$
    b. $2n^4 + 5n^3 + 15n - 2$
    c. $9n^4 + 8n^3 + 15n$
    d. $2n^4 + 8n^3 + 15n + 3$

42. Multiply $1,987 \times 0.05$.
    e. 9.935
    f. 99.35
    g. 993.5
    h. 999.35

43. What is the product of the following expression?

$$(4x - 8)(5x^2 + x + 6)$$

    a. $20x^3 - 36x^2 + 16x - 48$
    b. $6x^3 - 41x^2 + 12x + 15$
    c. $20x^3 + 11x^2 - 37x - 12$
    d. $2x^3 - 11x^2 - 32x + 20$

44. For the following similar triangles, what are the values of x and y (rounded to one decimal place)?

 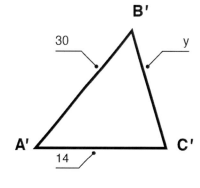

    e. $x = 16.5, y = 25.1$
    f. $x = 19.5, y = 24.1$
    g. $x = 17.1, y = 26.3$
    h. $x = 26.3, y = 17.1$

45. A solution needs 5 mL of saline for every 8 mL of medicine given. How much saline is needed for 45 mL of medicine?
    a. $\frac{225}{8}$ mL
    b. 72 mL
    c. 28 mL
    d. $\frac{45}{8}$ mL

46. If the volume of a sphere is 288π cubic meters, what are the radius and surface area of the same sphere?

    e. Radius: 6 meters, Surface Area: 144π square meters
    f. Radius: 36 meters, Surface Area: 144π square meters
    g. Radius: 6 meters, Surface Area: 12π square meters
    h. Radius: 36 meters, Surface Area: 12π square meters

47. The width of a rectangular house is 22 feet. What is the perimeter of this house if it has the same area as a house that is 33 feet wide and 50 feet long?

    a. 184 feet
    b. 200 feet
    c. 194 feet
    d. 206 feet

48. How much more area is covered by the rectangle than by the triangle?

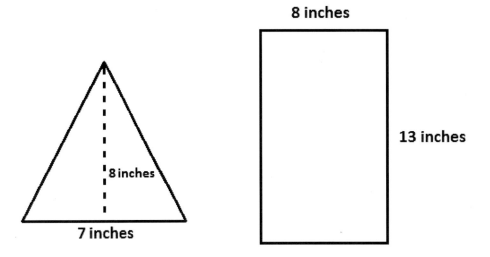

    e. 48
    f. 21
    g. 104
    h. 76

49. How will the following number be written in standard form: $(1 \times 10^4) + (3 \times 10^3) + (7 \times 10^1) + (8 \times 10^0)$

    a. 137
    b. 13,078
    c. 1,378
    d. 8,731

50. If $3x = 6y = -2z = 24$, then what does $4xy + z$ equal?

    e. 116
    f. 130
    g. 84
    h. 108

51. Johnny earns $2,334.50 from his job each month. He pays $1,437 for monthly expenses. Johnny is planning a vacation in 3 months that he estimates will cost $1,750 total. How much will Johnny have left over from three months of saving once he pays for his vacation?
    a. $948.50
    b. $584.50
    c. $852.50
    d. $942.50

52. What is the value of the expression: $7^2 - 3 \times (4 + 2) + 15 \div 5$?
    e. 12.2
    f. 40.2
    g. 34
    h. 58.2

53. Which of the following is largest?
    a. 0.45
    b. 0.096
    c. 0.3
    d. 0.313

54. Which of the following is NOT a way to write 40 percent of N?
    e. $(0.4)N$

    f. $\frac{2}{5}N$

    g. $40N$

    h. $\frac{4N}{10}$

55. Which is closest to 17.8×9.9?
    a. 140
    b. 180
    c. 200
    d. 350

56. What is $\frac{420}{98}$ rounded to the nearest integer?
    e. 4
    f. 3
    g. 5
    h. 6

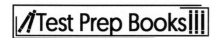
57. 16. A closet is filled with red, blue, and green shirts. If $\frac{1}{3}$ of the shirts are green and $\frac{2}{5}$ are red, what fraction of the shirts are blue?

    a. $\frac{4}{15}$

    b. $\frac{1}{5}$

    c. $\frac{7}{15}$

    d. $\frac{1}{2}$

58. If $2x + 6 = 20$, what is x?

    e.   3
    f.   4
    g.   7
    h.   9

59. Apples cost $2 each, while oranges cost $3 each. Maria purchased 10 fruits in total and spent $22. How many apples did she buy?

    a.   5
    b.   6
    c.   7
    d.   8

60. What are the polynomial roots of $x^2 + x - 2$?

    e.   1 and -2
    f.   -1 and 2
    g.   2 and -2
    h.   9 and 13

61. Which measure for the center of a small sample set is most affected by outliers?

    a.   Mean
    b.   Median
    c.   Mode
    d.   Range

62. Given the value of a given stock at monthly intervals, which graph should be used to best represent the trend of the stock?

    e.   Box plot
    f.   Line plot
    g.   Scatter plot
    h.   Line graph

63. Gary is driving home to see his parents for Christmas. He travels at a constant speed of 60 miles per hour for a total of 350 miles. How many minutes will it take him to travel home if he takes a break for 10 minutes every 100 miles?

64. Kelly is selling cookies to raise money for the chorus. She has 500 cookies to sell. At the first lunch, she sells 45% of the cookies to the sixth graders. At the second lunch, she sells 40% of what's left to the seventh graders. If she sells 60% of the remaining cookies to the eighth graders, how many cookies does Kelly have left at the end of all lunches?

65. Find the value of x. Assume the two horizontal lines are parallel.

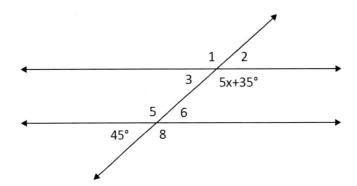

66. What is the value of the following expression?

$$\sqrt{8^2 + 6^2}$$

67. $864 \div 36 =$

Answer Explanations for Practice Test #1

Editing/Revising

1. D: The problem in the original sentence is that the second sentence is a dependent clause that cannot stand alone as a sentence; it must be attached to the main clause found in the first sentence. Because the main clause comes first, it does not need to be separated by a comma. However, if the dependent clause came first, then a comma would be necessary, which is why Choice *C* is incorrect. *A* and *B* also insert unnecessary commas into the sentence.

2. H: Choice *H* is correct because it uses correct parallel structure of plural nouns. *E* is incorrect because the word *shoe* should not be in singular form. Choice *F* is incorrect; semicolons are used in lists only if there is a list within a list. Choice *G* is incorrect because it pluralizes *makeup*, which is already in plural form.

3. C: The possessive form of the word "it" is "its." The contraction "it's" denotes "it is." Therefore, Choice *C* is correct. Choice *A* is incorrect because the end punctuation should be inside the quotes. Choice *B* is incorrect because removed the comma would create a run-on sentence. Distinguishes is the correct tense of the verb so Choice *D* is also incorrect.

4. F: Sentence 2 should be corrected to reflect the verb tense of the rest of the passage which is past tense. *Towards the end of his career, Carver returned to his first love of art.*

5. C: The next paragraph states that "These advanced offices oftentimes require a Professional Engineering (PE) license which can be obtained through additional college courses, professional experience, and acceptable scores on the Fundamentals of Engineering (FE) and Professional Engineering (PE) standardized assessments." Since the word *oftentimes* is used instead of *always*, Choice *C* is the best response.

6. G: The best answer is Choice *G*. Items in a list should be separated by a comma. Choice *E* is incorrect because there are no commas within the list to separate the items. Choice *F* is incorrect; a semicolon is used in a series only when a comma is present within the list itself. Choice *H* is incorrect because the conjunction *and* is missing before the word *calculus*.

7. A: The sentence is correct as-is. The words *one* and *bachelor* have apostrophe *-s* at the end because they show possession for the words that come after. The other answer choices do not indicate possession is being shown.

8. H: To begin, *of* is not required here. *Apprenticeship* is also more appropriate in this context than *apprentice opportunities*; *apprentice* describes an individual in an apprenticeship, not an apprenticeship itself. Both of these changes are needed, making Choice *H* the correct answer.

9. D: Choice *D* is correct because it breaks the section into coherent sentences and emphasizes the main point the author is trying to communicate: the PE license is required for some higher positions, it's obtained by scoring well on the two standardized assessments, and college and experience can be used to prepare for the assessments in order to gain the certification. The original sentence is a run-on and contains confusing information, so Choice *A* is incorrect. Choice *B* fixes the run-on aspect, but the

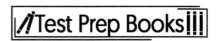

sentence is indirect and awkward in construction. Choice *C* is incorrect for the same reason as Choice *B*, and it is a run on.

10. F: *Once the job begins, this line of work* is the best way to phrase this sentence. Choice *E* is incorrect because *lines* does not match up with *this*; it would instead match up with the word *these*. Choice *G* is incorrect; *these line* should say *this line*. Choice *H* is incorrect; *job begin* is faulty subject/verb agreement.

11. A: The word is spelled correctly as it is: *expertise*.

12. G: *Allows* is inappropriate because it does not stress what those in the position of aircraft engineers actually need to be able to do. *Requires* is the only alternative that fits because it actually describes necessary skills of the job.

13. D: The words *equations* and *processes* in this sentence should be plural. Choices *A, B,* and *C* have one or both words as singular, which is incorrect.

14. E: The correct response is Choice *E* because this statement's intent is to give examples as to how aircraft engineers apply mathematical equations and scientific processes towards aeronautical and aerospace issues and/or inventions. The answer is not *Therefore*, Choice *F*, or *Furthermore*, Choice *H*, because no causality is being made between ideas. Two items are neither being compared nor contrasted, so *However*, Choice *G*, is also not the correct answer.

15. A: No change is required. The comma is properly placed after the introductory phrase *In May of 2015*. Choice *B* is missing the word *In*. Choice *C* does not separate the introductory phrase from the rest of the sentence. Choice *D* places an extra comma prior to 2015.

16. E: The word *conversely* best demonstrates the opposite sentiments in this passage. Choice *F* is incorrect because it denotes agreement with the previous statement. Choice *G* is incorrect because the sentiment is not restated but opposed. Choice *H* is incorrect because the previous statement is not a cause for the sentence in question.

17. A: The correct answer is Choice *A*, *are projected*. The present tense *are* matches with the rest of the sentence. The verb *are* also matches with the plural *employment opportunities*. Choice *B* uses *will be projected*, which is incorrect because the statistic is being used as evidence, which demands a present or past tense verb. In this case it is present tense to maintain consistency. Choice *C* is incorrect because the singular verb *is* does not match with the plural subject *employment opportunities*. Choice *D* is incorrect because the past tense verb *were* does not maintain consistency with the present tense in the rest of the passage.

18. G: Choice *G* is the best answer because introductory words like "Nevertheless" are always succeeded by a comma.

19. D: The main subject and verb in this sentence are far apart from each other. The subject is *engineers* and the subject is *are projected*. Although there is a clause which interrupts the subject and the verb, they still must agree with each other.

20. H: The correct phrase should be "War on Terror." The phrase is capitalized because it was part of the campaign phrase that was launched by the U.S. government after September 11. Punctuation should always be used inside double quotes as well, making Choice *H* the best answer.

21. C: Choice *A* is incorrect because the subject *Terrorists* is plural while the verb *uses* is singular, so the subject and verb do not agree with each other. Choice *B* is incorrect because the apostrophe in the word *Terrorist's* shows possession. Choice *D* is incorrect because the word *achieves* should be *achieve*.

22. E: No change is needed. Choices *F* and *G* utilize incorrect comma placements. Choice *H* utilizes an incorrect verb tense (*responding*).

23. B: The best answer Choice is *B*, *who live mainly in South and Southwest Asia*. The directional terms *South Asia* and *Southwest Asia* are integral parts of a proper name and should therefore be capitalized.

24. H: The apostrophe in *America's* shows possession of the word *support*, and *Israel* should be capitalized because it is a country and therefore a proper noun. Choice *E* does not show possession in the word *Americas*. Choice *F* does not capitalize the word *Israel*. Choice *G* does not show possession and does not include the necessary comma at the end of the phrase.

25. A: The verb should be in the past tense—the other three answer choices either have a present or continuous verb tense, so these are incorrect.

Reading Comprehension

26. H: Choice *H* correctly summarizes Frost's theme of life's journey and the choices one makes. While Choice *E* can be seen as an interpretation, it is a literal one and is incorrect. Literal is not symbolic. Choice *F* presents the idea of good and evil as a theme, and the poem does not specify this struggle for the traveler. Choice *G* is a similarly incorrect answer. Love is not the theme.

27. C: Line 5 states, " Because it was grassy and wanted wear". The grass was taller and had not been trampled down by many travelers. The other choices are not lines that directly contribute to the idea that the second path was less traveled.

28. H: Context clues indicate that Choice *H* is correct because the passage provides great detail on Mr. Utterson's feelings about locating Hyde. Choice *E* does not fit because there is no mention of Mr. Lanyon's mental state. Choice *F* is incorrect; although the text does make mention of bells, Choice *B* is not the *best* answer overall. Choice *G* is incorrect because the passage states that Mr. Utterson was determined, not unsure.

29. A: The word *city* appears in the passage several times, thus establishing the location for the reader.

30. F: The passage states that the Juggernaut causes the children to scream. Choices *E* and *H* don't apply because the text doesn't mention either of these instances specifically. Choice *G* is incorrect because there is nothing in the text that mentions space travel.

31. B: The mention of *morning*, *noon*, and *night* make it clear that the word *haunt* refers to frequent appearances at various times. Choice *A* doesn't work because the text makes no mention of levitating. Choices *C* and *D* are not correct because the text makes mention of Mr. Utterson's anguish and

148

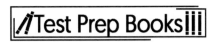

disheartenment because of his failure to find Hyde but does not make mention of Mr. Utterson's feelings negatively affecting anyone else.

32. H: Choice *H* is the correct answer because of the repetition of the *L*-words. Hyperbole is an exaggeration, so Choice *E* doesn't work. No comparison is being made, so no simile or juxtaposition is being used, thus eliminating Choices *F* and *G*.

33. D: The speaker invokes the game of hide and seek to indicate they will continue their search for Hyde. Choices *A* and *B* are not possible answers because the text doesn't refer to any name changes or an identity crisis, despite Mr. Utterson's extreme obsession with finding Hyde. The text also makes no mention of a mistaken identity when referring to Hyde, so Choice *C* is also incorrect.

34. G: Gulliver becomes acquainted with the people and practices of his new surroundings. Choice *G* is the correct answer because it most extensively summarizes the entire passage. While Choices *E* and *F* are reasonable possibilities, they reference portions of Gulliver's experiences, not the whole. Choice *H* is incorrect because Gulliver doesn't express repentance or sorrow in this particular passage.

35. A: Principal refers to *chief* or *primary* within the context of this text. Choice *A* is the answer that most closely aligns with this definition. Choices *B* and *D* make reference to a helper or follower while Choice *C* doesn't meet the description of Reldresal from the passage.

36. G: One can reasonably infer that Gulliver is considerably larger than the children who were playing around him because multiple children could fit into his hand. Choice *F* is incorrect because there is no indication of stress in Gulliver's tone. Choices *E* and *H* aren't the best answer because though Gulliver seems fond of his new acquaintances, he didn't travel there with the intentions of meeting new people or to express a definite love for them in this particular portion of the text.

37. C: The emperor made a *definitive decision* to expose Gulliver to their native customs. In this instance, the word *mind* was not related to a vote, question, or cognitive ability.

38. E: Choice *E* is correct. This assertion does *not* support the fact that games are a commonplace event in this culture because it mentions conduct, not games. Choices *F*, *G*, and *H* are incorrect because these do support the fact that games were a commonplace event.

39. B: Choice *B* is the only option that mentions the correlation between physical ability and leadership positions. Choices *A* and *D* are unrelated to physical strength and leadership abilities. Choice *C* does not make a deduction that would lead to the correct answer—it only comments upon the abilities of common townspeople.

40. F: It is apparent that Lincoln is referring to a period of time within the context of the passage because the sentence contains the words *years* and *ago*. Choices *E*, *G*, and *H* do not fit the language or context of the sentence and are therefore incorrect.

41. C: Lincoln's reference to *the brave men, living and dead, who struggled here,* proves that he is referring to a battlefield. Choices *A* and *B* are incorrect, as a *civil war* is mentioned and not a war with France or a war in the Sahara Desert. Choice *D* is incorrect because it does not make sense to consecrate a President's ground instead of a battlefield ground for soldiers who died during the American Civil War.

42. H: Abraham Lincoln is the former president of the United States, and he references a "civil war" during his address.

43. A: Lincoln doesn't address any of the topics outlined in Choices *B, C,* or *D.* Therefore, Choice *A* is the correct answer.

44. H: Choice *H* is the correct answer because of the repetition of the word *people* at the end of the passage. Choice *E, antimetabole,* is the repetition of words in a succession. Choice *F, antiphrasis,* is a form of denial of an assertion in a text. Choice *G, anaphora,* is the repetition that occurs at the beginning of sentences.

45. A: Choice *A* is correct because Lincoln's intention was to memorialize the soldiers who had fallen as a result of war as well as celebrate those who had put their lives in danger for the sake of their country. Choices *B, C,* and *D* are incorrect because Lincoln's speech was supposed to foster a sense of pride among the members of the audience while connecting them to the soldiers' experiences.

46. G: In lines 6 and 7, it is stated that avarice can prevent a man from being necessitously poor, but it also makes him too timorous, or fearful, to be wealthy. Choice *E* is incorrect because avarice prevents a man from being poor. Choice *F* is incorrect because the passage states that oppression, not avarice, is the consequence of wealth. Choice *H* is incorrect because the passage does not state that avarice drives a person's desire to be wealthy.

47. D: Paine believes that the distinction that is beyond a natural or religious reason is between king and subjects. Choice *A* is incorrect because he states that the distinction between good and bad is made in heaven. Choice *B* is incorrect because he states that the distinction between male and female is natural. Choice *C* is incorrect because he does not mention anything about the distinction between humans and animals.

48. E: The passage states that the Heathens were the first to introduce government by kings into the world. Choice *F* is incorrect because the quiet lives of patriarchs came before the Heathens introduced this type of government and Paine puts it in opposition to government by kings. Choice *G* is incorrect because it was Christians, not Heathens, who paid divine honors to living kings. Heathens honored deceased kings. Choice *H* is incorrect because, while equal rights of nature are mentioned in the paragraph, they are not mentioned in relation to the Heathens.

49. B: Paine asserts that a monarchy is against the equal rights of nature and cites several parts of scripture that also denounce it. He doesn't say it is against the laws of nature. Because he uses scripture to further his argument, it is not despite scripture that he denounces the monarchy. Paine addresses the law by saying the courts also do not support a monarchical government.

50. E: To be *idolatrous* is to worship someone or something other than God, in this case, kings. Choice *F* is incorrect because it is not defined as being deceitful. Choice *G* is incorrect because, while idolatry is considered a sin, it is an example of a sin, not a synonym for it. Choice *H* is incorrect because, while idolatry may have been considered illegal in some cultures, it is not a definition for the term.

51. A: The tone is incredulous. While contemplative is an option because of the inquisitive nature of the text, Choice *A* is correct because Frederick Douglass is astonished that he, a former slave, would be called upon to celebrate liberty that was not extended to him or to others of his race. Choice *B* is incorrect because Frederick Douglass is drawing contrasts between two groups of people rather than

150

being inclusive. Choice *C* is incorrect because Frederick Douglass is expressing strong emotion, incredulity, rather than contemplation. Choice *D* is incorrect because Frederick Douglass is not nonchalant, nor accepting of the circumstances which he describes.

52. G: Choice *G*, *contented*, is the only word that has the opposite meaning of *obdurate*. Therefore, Choices *E*, *F*, and *H* are incorrect.

53. B: While the speaker makes biblical references, it is not the main focus of the passage, thus eliminating Choice *A* as an answer. The passage also makes no mention of wealthy landowners and doesn't speak of any positive response to the historical events, so Choices *C* and *D* are not correct.

54: H: Choice *H* is the correct answer because it clearly makes reference to justice being denied.

55: D: It is an example of hyperbole. Choices *A* and *B* are unrelated. Assonance is the repetition of sounds and commonly occurs in poetry. Parallelism refers to two statements that correlate in some manner. Choice *C* is incorrect because amplification normally refers to clarification of meaning by broadening the sentence structure, while hyperbole refers to a phrase or statement that is being exaggerated.

56: G: Recognize the equivocation of the speaker and those that he represents. Choice *G* is correct because the speaker is clear about his intention and stance throughout the text. Choice *E* could be true, but the words "common text" is arguable. Choice *F* is also partially true, as another group of people affected by slavery are being referenced. However, the speaker is not trying to convince the audience that injustices have been committed, as it is already understood there have been injustices committed. Choice *H* is also close to the correct answer, but it is not the *best* answer choice possible.

57. D: The use of "I" could have all of the effects for the reader; it could serve to have a "hedging" effect, allow the reader to connect with the author in a more personal way, and cause the reader to empathize more with the egrets. However, it doesn't distance the reader from the text, thus eliminating Choice *D*.

58. G: The quote provides an example of a warden protecting one of the colonies. Choice *E* is incorrect because the speaker of the quote is a warden, not a hunter. Choice *F* is incorrect because the quote does not lighten the mood but shows the danger of the situation between the wardens and the hunters. Choice *H* is incorrect because there is no humor found in the quote.

59. D: A *rookery* is a colony of breeding birds. Although *rookery* could mean Choice *A*, houses in a slum area, it does not make sense in this context. Choices *B* and *C* are both incorrect, as this is not a place for hunters to trade tools or for wardens to trade stories.

60. F: The previous sentence is describing "twenty colonies" of birds, so what follows should be a bird colony. Choice *E* may be true, but we have no evidence of this in the text. Choice *G* does touch on the tension between the hunters and wardens, but there is no official "Bird Island Battle" mentioned in the text. Choice *H* does not exist in the text.

61. D: The text mentions several different times how and why the association has been successful and gives examples to back this fact. Choice *A* is incorrect because although the article, in some instances, calls certain people to act, it is not the purpose of the entire passage. There is no way to tell if Choices *B* and *C* are correct, as they are not mentioned in the text.

62. G: Choice *E* might be true in a general sense, but it is not relevant to the context of the text. Choice *F* is incorrect because the hunters are not studying lines of flight to help wardens, but to hunt birds. Choice *H* is incorrect because nothing in the text mentions that hunters are trying to build homes underneath lines of flight of birds for good luck.

63. A: The passage's purpose is to introduce certain insects that transition from water to air. Choice *B* is incorrect because although the passage talks about gills, it is not the central idea of the passage. Choices *C* and *D* are incorrect because the passage does not "define" or "invite," but only serves as an introduction to stoneflies, dragonflies, and mayflies and their transition from water to air.

64. G: The act of shedding part or all of the outer shell. Choices *E*, *F*, and *H* are incorrect.

65. B: Notice how the first paragraph goes into detail describing how insects are able to breathe air. The second paragraph acts as a contrast to the first by stating "[i]t is of great interest to find that, nevertheless, a number of insects spend much of their time under water." Watch for transition words such as "nevertheless" to help find what type of passage you're dealing with.

66. G: The early stages in between periods of molting are acted out in the water, while the last stage is in the air. Choices *E, F,* and *H* are all incorrect. *Instars* is the phase between two periods of molting, and the text explains when these transitions occur.

67. C: Overall, the author presents us with information on the subject. One moment where personal interest is depicted is when the author states, "It is of great interest to find that, nevertheless, a number of insects spend much of their time under water."

Math

1. B: First, subtract 4 from each side. This yields $6t = 12$. Now, divide both sides by 6 to obtain $t = 2$.

2. F: To be directly proportional means that $y = kx$. If x is changed from 5 to 20, the value of x is multiplied by 4. Applying the same rule to the y-value, also multiply the value of y by 4. Therefore:

$$y = 12$$

3. B: From the slope-intercept form, $y = mx + b$, it is known that b is the y-intercept, which is 1. Compute the slope as $\frac{2-1}{1-0} = 1$, so the equation is $y = x + 1$.

4. E: Each bag contributes $4x + 1$ treats. The total treats will be in the form $4nx + n$ where n is the total number of bags. The total is in the form $60x + 15$, from which it is known $n = 15$.

5. B: Audit and Taxation Services total income is unknown (we can call it ATS) and its percentage of overall income is 40%+30%=70%. Accounting Services income is $100,000, which makes up 20% of overall income. We can use these dollar amounts and percentages to set up a proportion:

$$\frac{ATS}{\$100,000} = \frac{70}{20}$$

We can solve this equation to find Audit and Taxation Services income:

$$ATS = \left(\frac{70}{20}\right)\$100,000 = \$350,000$$

6. E: Finding the roots means finding the values of x when y is zero. The quadratic formula could be used, but in this case, it is possible to factor by hand, since the numbers -1 and 2 add to 1 and multiply to -2. So, factor $x^2 + x - 2 = (x-1)(x+2) = 0$, then set each factor equal to zero. Solving for each value gives the values $x = 1$ and $x = -2$.

7. C: To find the y-intercept, substitute zero for x, which gives us:

$$y = 0^{\frac{5}{3}} + (0 - 3)(0 + 1) = 0 + (-3)(1) = -3$$

8. H: The slope from this equation is 50, and it is interpreted as the cost per gigabyte used. Since the g-value represents number of gigabytes and the equation is set equal to the cost in dollars, the slope relates these two values. For every gigabyte used on the phone, the bill goes up 50 dollars.

9. A: Simplify this to:

$$(4x^2y^4)^{\frac{3}{2}} = 4^{\frac{3}{2}}(x^2)^{\frac{3}{2}}(y^4)^{\frac{3}{2}}$$

$$4^{\frac{3}{2}} = (\sqrt{4})^3 = 2^3 = 8$$

For the other, recall that the exponents must be multiplied; this yields:

$$8x^{2\cdot\frac{3}{2}}y^{4\cdot\frac{3}{2}} = 8x^3y^6$$

10. F: Start by squaring both sides to get $1 + x = 16$. Then subtract 1 from both sides to get $x = 15$.

11. C: Multiply both sides by x to get $x + 2 = 2x$. Subtract x from both sides to get $x = 2$.

12. E: Parallel lines have the same slope. The slope of the given equation is 3. The slope of Choice G can be seen to be $\frac{1}{3}$ by dividing both sides by 3. The other choices are in standard form $Ax + By = C$, for

153

which the slope is given by $\frac{-A}{B}$. For Choice *E*, the equation can be written as $6x - 2y = -2$. Therefore, the slope is:

$$\frac{-A}{B} = \frac{-6}{-2} = 3$$

This is the same as the given equation. The slope of Choice *F* is:

$$\frac{-A}{B} = \frac{-4}{-1} = 4$$

The slope of Choice *F* is 4. The slope of Choice *H* is:

$$\frac{-A}{B} = \frac{-2}{-2} = 1$$

13. D: Denote the width as w and the length as l. Then, $l = 3w + 5$. The perimeter is $2w + 2l = 90$. Substituting the first expression for l into the second equation yields:

$$2(3w + 5) + 2w = 90$$

$$6w + 10 + 2w = 90$$

$$8w = 80$$

$$w = 10$$

Putting this into the first equation, it yields:

$$l = 3(10) + 5 = 35$$

14. E: Putting the scores in order from least to greatest, we have 60, 75, 80, and 85, as well as one unknown. The median is 80, so 80 must be the middle data point out of these five. Therefore, the unknown data point must be the fourth or fifth data point, meaning it must be greater than or equal to 80. The only answer that fails to meet this condition is 60.

15. B: If 60% of 50 workers are women, then there are 30 women working in the office. If half of them are wearing skirts, then that means 15 women wear skirts. Since none of the men wear skirts, this means there are 15 people wearing skirts.

16. E: Let the unknown score be x. The average will be:

$$\frac{5 \times 50 + 4 \times 70 + x}{10} = \frac{530 + x}{10} = 55$$

Multiply both sides by 10 to get $530 + x = 550$, or $x = 20$.

17. D: For manufacturing costs, there is a linear relationship between the cost to the company and the number produced, with a y-intercept given by the base cost of acquiring the means of production and a slope given by the cost to produce one unit. In this case, that base cost is $50,000, while the cost per unit is $40. So:

$$y = 40x + 50,000$$

18. G: A die has an equal chance for each outcome. Since it has six sides, each outcome has a probability of $\frac{1}{6}$. The chance of a 1 or a 2 is therefore:

$$\frac{1}{6} + \frac{1}{6} = \frac{1}{3}$$

19. A: The slope is given by:

$$m = \frac{y_2 - y_1}{x_2 - x_1} = \frac{0 - 4}{0 - (-3)} = -\frac{4}{3}$$

20. F: An equilateral triangle has three sides of equal length, so if the total perimeter is 18 feet, each side must be 6 feet long. A square with sides of 6 feet will have an area of $6^2 = 36$ square feet.

21. A: 3.6. Divide 3 by 5 to get 0.6 and add that to the whole number 3, to get 3.6. An alternative is to incorporate the whole number 3 earlier on by creating an improper fraction:

$$\frac{18}{5}$$

Then divide 18 by 5 to get 3.6.

22. G: 9 Cars. The average is calculated by adding up each month's sales and dividing the sum by the total number of months in the time period. Dealer 1 sold 2 cars in July, 12 in August, 8 in September, 6 in October, 10 in November, and 15 in December. The sum of these sales is:

$$2 + 12 + 8 + 6 + 10 + 15 = 53 \text{ cars}$$

To find the average, this sum is divided by the total number of months, which is 6. When 53 is divided by 6, it yields 8.8333... Since cars are sold in whole numbers, the answer is rounded to 9 cars.

23. A: 6 boxes. The team needs a total of $270, and each box earns them $3. Therefore, the total number of boxes needed to be sold is $270 \div 3$, which is 90. With 15 people on the team, the total of 90 can be divided by 15, which equals 6. This means that each member of the team needs to sell 6 boxes for the team to raise enough money to buy new uniforms.

24. G: 30. A complete circle measures 360 degrees. This circle is broken up into 4 different parts with different measures for each part. Adding these parts should give a total of 360 degrees. The equation generated from this diagram is:

$$4x + 5x + x + 2x = 360$$

Collecting like terms gives the equation $12x = 360$, which can be solved by dividing by 12 to give $x = 30$. The value of x in the diagram is 30.

25. D: $\frac{1}{12}$. The probability of picking the winner of the race is $\frac{1}{4}$, or $\left(\frac{\text{number of favorable outcomes}}{\text{number of total outcomes}}\right)$. Assuming the winner was picked on the first selection, three horses remain from which to choose the runner-up (these are dependent events). Therefore, the probability of picking the runner-up is $\frac{1}{3}$. To determine the probability of multiple events, the probability of each event is multiplied:

$$\frac{1}{4} \times \frac{1}{3} = \frac{1}{12}$$

26. G: A full rotation is 360 degrees. Taking the total degrees that the figure skater spins and dividing by 360 yields 6.25. She spins 6 total times and then one-quarter of a turn more. This quarter of a turn to her right means she ends up facing east.

27. C: The sum of all angles in a polygon with n sides is found by the expression $(n - 2) \times 180$. Since this polygon has 5 sides, the total degrees of the interior angles can be found using the equation:

$$(5 - 2) \times 180 = 540$$

Adding up each of the given angles yields a total of:

$$111 + 113 + 92 + 128 = 444 \text{ degrees}$$

Taking the total of 540 degrees and subtracting the given sum of 444 degrees gives a missing value of 96 degrees for the measure of angle P.

28. E: The expression in the denominator can be factored into the two binomials:

$$(x - 4)(x - 2)$$

Once the expression is rewritten as $\frac{x-4}{(x-4)(x-2)}$, we can see that the values of $x = 4$ and $x = 2$ result in a denominator with a value of 0. Since 0 cannot be in the denominator of a fraction, the expression is undefined at the values of $x = 2, 4$.

29. A: The total number of coins in the jar is 86. Of these, 31 are nickels or quarters (which means they are not pennies or dimes). The probability of Nina drawing a coin that is not a penny or a dime is $\frac{31}{86} \approx 0.36$.

30. G: For the first car, the trip will be 450 miles at 18 miles to the gallon. The total gallons needed for this car will be:

$$450 \div 18 = 25$$

For the second car, the trip will be 450 miles at 25 miles to the gallon, or $450 \div 25 = 18$, which will require 18 gallons of gas. Adding these two amounts of gas gives a total of 43 gallons of gas. If the gas costs $2.49 per gallon, the cost of the trip for both cars is:

$$43 \times \$2.49 = \$107.07$$

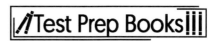

31. C: $\frac{4}{3}$

Set up the problem and find a common denominator for both fractions.

$$\frac{14}{33} + \frac{10}{11}$$

Multiply each fraction across by 1 to convert to a common denominator

$$\frac{14}{33} \times \frac{1}{1} + \frac{10}{11} \times \frac{3}{3}$$

Once over the same denominator, add across the top. The total is over the common denominator.

$$\frac{14 + 30}{33} = \frac{44}{33}$$

Reduce by dividing both numerator and denominator by 11.

$$\frac{44 \div 11}{33 \div 11} = \frac{4}{3}$$

32. F: This question involves the percent formula.

$$\frac{32}{x} = \frac{25}{100}$$

We multiply the diagonal numbers, 32 and 100, to get 3,200. Dividing by the remaining number, 25, gives us 128.

The percent formula does not have to be used for a question like this. Since 25% is $\frac{1}{4}$ of 100, you know that 32 needs to be multiplied by 4, which yields 128.

33. D: The first step in solving this equation is to collect like terms on the left side of the equation. This yields the new equation:

$$-4 + 8x = 8 - 10x$$

The next step is to move the x terms to one side by adding $10x$ to both sides, making the equation:

$$-4 + 18x = 8$$

Then the -4 can be moved to the right side of the equation to form:

$$18x = 12$$

Dividing both sides of the equation by 18 gives a value of 0.67, or $\frac{2}{3}$.

34. F: This triangle is a right triangle because it has a right-angle measure in the corner. The Pythagorean theorem can be used to find the missing side lengths. The Pythagorean theorem states that $a^2 + b^2 = c^2$, where c is the hypotenuse and a and b are the other two side lengths. The hypotenuse, c, is $12.6 +$

22. $4 = 35$. One side, a, is 21 (since we were told that $y = 21$), and for the remaining side, b, we can use our variable x. Plugging these values into the equation forms:

$$21^2 + x^2 = 35^2$$

Squaring both given numbers and subtracting them yields the equation:

$$x^2 = 784$$

so,

$$x = \sqrt{784} = 28.$$

35. A: The first step is to find the equation of the line that is perpendicular to $y = 2x - 3$ and passes through the point $(0, 5)$. The slope of a perpendicular line is the negative reciprocal of the original slope, and since our original slope is 2, the new slope is $-\frac{1}{2}$. The y-intercept is the value of y when $x = 0$, and since we know $(0,5)$ is on the new line, our new y-intercept is 5. The new equation is:

$$y = -\frac{1}{2}x + 5$$

In order to find which points lie on the new line, we can substitute each choice's x and y values into the equation to determine whether they form a true statement. For A, the equation $4 = -\frac{1}{2}(2) + 5$ makes a true statement, so the point $(2, 4)$ lies on the line.

For B, the equation $7 = -\frac{1}{2}(-2) + 5$ makes the statement $7 = 6$, which is not a true statement. Therefore, B is not a point that lies on the line. For C, the equation $-3 = -\frac{1}{2}(4) + 5$ becomes $-3 = 3$ which is not a true statement, so the point $(4, -3)$ is not on the line.

For the last point in D, the equation $10 = -\frac{1}{2}(-6) + 5$ makes the statement $10 = 8$. This is not a true statement, so the point $(-6, 10)$ does not lie on the line.

36. F: To factor $x^2 + 4x + 4$, the numbers needed are those that add to 4 and multiply to 4. Therefore, both numbers must be 2, and the expression factors to:

$$x^2 + 4x + 4 = (x + 2)^2$$

Similarly, the expression factors to $x^2 - x - 6 = (x - 3)(x + 2)$, so that they have $x + 2$ in common.

37. D: This problem involves a composition function, where one function is plugged into the other function. In this case, the $f(x)$ function is plugged into the $g(x)$ function for each x value. Since $f(x) = 2$, the composition equation becomes:

$$g\big(f(x)\big) = g(2) = (2)^3 - 3(2)^2 - 2(2) + 6$$

Simplifying the equation gives the answer:

$$g(f(x)) = 8 - 3(4) - 2(2) + 6$$

$$g(f(x)) = 8 - 12 - 4 + 6 = -2$$

$$g(f(x)) = -2$$

38. F: 100 cm is equal to 1 m. 1.3 divided by 100 is 0.013. Therefore, 1.3 cm is equal to 0.013 m. Because 1 cm is equal to 10 mm, 1.3 cm is equal to 13 mm.

39. B: 725

Set up the division problem.

$$1.4 \overline{)1015}$$

Move the decimal over one place to the right in both numbers.

$$14 \overline{)10150}$$

14 does not go into 1 or 10 but does go into 101, so start there.

$$
\begin{array}{r}
725 \\
14\overline{)10150} \\
-\ 98 \\
\hline
35 \\
-\ 28 \\
\hline
70 \\
-\ 70 \\
\hline
0
\end{array}
$$

The result is 725.

40. H: This system of equations involves one quadratic function and one linear function, as seen from the degree of each equation. One way to solve this is through substitution.

Solving for y in the second equation yields:

$$y = x + 2$$

Plugging this equation in for the y of the quadratic equation yields:

$$x^2 - 2x + x + 2 = 8$$

Simplifying the equation, it becomes:

$$x^2 - x + 2 = 8$$

159

Setting this equal to zero and factoring, it becomes:

$$x^2 - x - 6 = 0 = (x - 3)(x + 2)$$

Solving these two factors for x gives the zeros:

$$x = 3, -2$$

To find the y-value for the point, each number can be plugged in to either original equation. Solving each one for y yields the points $(3, 5)$ and $(-2, 0)$.

41. D: The expression is simplified by collecting like terms. Terms with the same variable and exponent are like terms, and their coefficients can be added.

42. F: 99.35. Set up the problem, with the larger number on top. Multiply as if there are no decimal places. Add the answer rows together. Count the number of decimal places that were in the original numbers (2).

Place the decimal in that many spots from the right for the final solution.

43. A: Finding the product means distributing one polynomial to the other so that each term in the first is multiplied by each term in the second. Then, like terms can be collected. Multiplying the factors yields the expression:

$$20x^3 + 4x^2 + 24x - 40x^2 - 8x - 48$$

Collecting like terms means adding the x^2 terms and adding the x terms. The final answer after simplifying the expression is:

$$20x^3 - 36x^2 + 16x - 48$$

44. G: Because the triangles are similar, the lengths of the corresponding sides are proportional. Therefore:

$$\frac{30 + x}{30} = \frac{22}{14} = \frac{y + 15}{y}$$

Using cross multiplication on the first two terms results in the equation:

$$14(30 + x) = 22 \times 30$$

When solved, this gives:

$$x \approx 17.1$$

Using cross multiplication on the last two terms results in the equation:

$$14(y + 15) = 22y$$

When solved, this gives:

$$y \approx 26.3$$

160

45. A: Every 8 mL of medicine requires 5 mL. The 45 mL first needs to be split into portions of 8 mL. This results in $\frac{45}{8}$ portions. Each portion requires 5 mL. Therefore, the following is necessary:

$$\frac{45}{8} \times 5 = \frac{45 \times 5}{8} = \frac{225}{8} \text{ mL}$$

46. E: Because the volume of the given sphere is 288π cubic meters, this gives:

$$\frac{4}{3}\pi r^3 = 288\pi$$

This equation is solved for r to obtain a radius of 6 meters. The formula for surface area is $4\pi r^2$, so:

$$SA = 4\pi 6^2 = 144\pi \text{ square meters}$$

47. C: First, find the area of the second house. The area is:

$$A = l \, x \, w = 33 \times 50 = 1{,}650 \text{ square feet}$$

Then, use the area formula to determine what length gives the first house an area of 1,650 square feet. So:

$$1{,}650 = 22 \times l$$

$$l = \frac{1{,}650}{22} = 75 \text{ feet}$$

Then, use the formula for perimeter to get:

$$75 + 75 + 22 + 22 = 194 \text{ feet}$$

48. H: First, find the area of both figures. We can use the formula for the area of a triangle ($A = \frac{1}{2}bh$) to find the area of this triangle:

$$\frac{1}{2}(7) \times x = 3.5x \text{ square inches}$$

The area of the rectangle is:

$$13 \times 8 = 104 \text{ square inches}$$

To find how much more area is covered by the square, the following equation can be used:

$$104 - 28 = 76$$

49. B: 13,078. The power of 10 by which a digit is multiplied corresponds with the number of zeros following the digit when expressing its value in standard form. Therefore:

$$(1 \times 10^4) + (3 \times 10^3) + (7 \times 10^1) + (8 \times 10^0)$$

$$10{,}000 + 3{,}000 + 70 + 8 = 13{,}078$$

161

50. E: First solve for *x, y,* and *z.* So:

$$3x = 24$$

$$x = 8$$

$$6y = 24$$

$$y = 4$$

$$-2z = 24$$

$$z = -12$$

This means the expression $4xy + z$ would be $4(8)(4) + (-12)$, which equals 116.

51. D: First, subtract $1,437 from $2,334.50 to find Johnny's monthly savings; this equals $897.50. Then, multiply this amount by 3 to find out how much he will have (in 3 months) before he pays for his vacation: this equals $2,692.50. Finally, subtract the cost of the vacation ($1,750) from this amount to find how much Johnny will have left: $942.50.

52. G: When performing calculations consisting of more than one operation, the order of operations should be followed: Parentheses, Exponents, Multiplication/Division, Addition/Subtraction.

Parentheses:

$$7^2 - 3 \times (4 + 2) + 15 \div 5$$

$$7^2 - 3 \times (6) + 15 \div 5$$

Exponents:

$$49 - 3 \times 6 + 15 \div 5$$

Multiplication/Division (from left to right):

$$49 - 18 + 3$$

Addition/Subtraction (from left to right):

$$49 - 18 + 3 = 34$$

53. A: Figure out which is largest by looking at the first non-zero digits. Choice *B*'s first non-zero digit is in the hundredths place. The other four all have non-zero digits in the tenths place, so it must be *A, C,* or *D.* Of these, *A* has the largest first non-zero digit.

54. G: $40N$ would be 4,000% of *N.* All of the other coefficients are equivalent to $\frac{40}{100}$ or 40%.

55. B: Instead of multiplying these out, the product can be estimated by using $18 \times 10 = 180$. The error here should be lower than 15, since it is rounded to the nearest integer, and the numbers add to something less than 30.

162

56. E: Dividing by 98 can be approximated by dividing by 100, which would mean shifting the decimal point of the numerator to the left by 2. The result is 4.2 and rounds to 4.

57. A: The total fraction taken up by green and red shirts will be:

$$\frac{1}{3} + \frac{2}{5} = \frac{5}{15} + \frac{6}{15} = \frac{11}{15}$$

The remaining fraction is:

$$1 - \frac{11}{15} = \frac{15}{15} - \frac{11}{15} = \frac{4}{15}$$

58. G: Begin by subtracting 6 from both sides to get $2x = 14$. Dividing both sides by 2 results in $x = 7$.

59. E: Let a be the number of apples and o the number of oranges. Then, the total cost is:

$$2a + 3o = 22$$

while it also known that $a + o = 10$. Using the knowledge of systems of equations, cancel the o-variables by multiplying the second equation by -3.

This makes the equation:

$$-3a - 3o = -30$$

Adding this to the first equation, the b-values cancel to get $-a = -8$, which simplifies to $a = 8$.

60. E: Finding the roots means finding the values of x when y is zero. The quadratic formula could be used, but in this case, it is possible to factor by hand, since the numbers -1 and 2 add to 1 and multiply to -2. So, factor:

$$x^2 + x - 2 = (x - 1)(x + 2) = 0$$

then set each factor equal to zero. Solving for each value gives the values $x = 1$ and $x = -2$.

61. A: Mean. An outlier is a data value that is either far above or far below the majority of values in a sample set. The mean is the average of all the values in the set. In a small sample set, a very high or very low number could drastically change the average of the data points. Outliers will have no more of an effect on the median (the middle value when arranged from lowest to highest) than any other value above or below the median. If the same outlier does not repeat, outliers will have no effect on the mode (value that repeats most often).

62. H: Line graph. The scenario involves data consisting of two variables, month and stock value. Box plots display data consisting of values for one variable. Therefore, a box plot is not an appropriate choice. Both line plots and circle graphs are used to display frequencies within categorical data. Neither can be used for the given scenario. Scatter plots compare the values of two variables to see if there are any patterns present. Line graphs display two numerical variables on a coordinate grid and show trends among the variables.

63. 380 minutes: To find the total driving time, the total distance of 350 miles can be divided by the constant speed of 60 miles per hour. This yields a time of 5.8333 hours, which is then rounded. Once the driving time is computed, the break times need to be found. If Gary takes a break for 10 minutes every 100 miles, he will take 3 breaks on his trip.

This will yield a total of 30 minutes of break time. Since the answer is needed in minutes, 5.8333 can be converted to minutes by multiplying by 60, giving a driving time of 350 minutes. Adding the break time of 30 minutes to the driving time of 350 minutes gives a total travel time of 380 minutes.

		3	8	0
(-)	(-)	(-)	(-)	(-)
	(.)	(.)	(.)	(.)
	(0)	(0)	(0)	(0)
	(1)	(1)	(1)	(1)
	(2)	(2)	(2)	(2)
	(3)	(3)	(3)	(3)
	(4)	(4)	(4)	(4)
	(5)	(5)	(5)	(5)
	(6)	(6)	(6)	(6)
	(7)	(7)	(7)	(7)
	(8)	(8)	(8)	(8)
	(9)	(9)	(9)	(9)

64. 66 Cookies: If the sixth graders bought 45% of the cookies, the number they bought is found by multiplying 0.45 by 500. They bought 225 cookies. The number of cookies left is:

$$500 - 225 = 275$$

During the second lunch, the seventh graders bought 40% of the cookies, which is found by multiplying 0.40 by the remaining 275 cookies. The seventh graders bought 110 cookies. This leaves 165 cookies to sell to the eighth graders. If they bought 60% of the remaining cookies, then they bought 99 cookies. Subtracting 99 from 165 cookies leaves Kelly with 66 cookies remaining after the three lunches.

```
          6 6
⊙ ⊙ ⊙ ⊙ ⊙
  ⊙ ⊙ ⊙ ⊙
0 0 0 0
1 1 1 1
2 2 2 2
3 3 3 3
4 4 4 4
5 5 5 5
6 6 ⑥ ⑥
7 7 7 7
8 8 8 8
9 9 9 9
```

65. 20: Because these are two parallel lines cut by a transversal, the angle with a measure of 45° is equal to the measure of angle 3. Angle 3 and the angle labeled $5x + 35°$ are supplementary angles (their sum is 180°), so

$$5x + 35° + 45° = 180°.$$

We can solve for x:

$$5x + 35° + 45° = 180°$$

$$5x + 80° = 180° \ 5$$

$$x = 100° \ x = 20°$$

```
          2 0
⊙ ⊙ ⊙ ⊙ ⊙
  ⊙ ⊙ ⊙ ⊙
0 0 0 ⓪
1 1 1 1
2 2 ② 2
3 3 3 3
4 4 4 4
5 5 5 5
6 6 6 6
7 7 7 7
8 8 8 8
9 9 9 9
```

66. 10: 8 squared is 64, and 6 squared is 36. These should be added together to get:

$$64 + 36 = 100$$

165

Then, the last step is to find the square root of 100, which is 10.

67. 24: The long division would be completed as follows:

$$
\begin{array}{r}
24 \\
36\overline{\smash{)}864} \\
-72\downarrow \\
\hline
144
\end{array}
$$

SHSAT Practice Tests #2, #3 & #4

To keep the size of this book manageable, save paper, and provide a digital test-taking experience, the 2nd, 3rd, and 4th practice tests can be found online. Scan the QR code or go to this link to access it:

testprepbooks.com/bonus/shsat

The first time you access the tests, you will need to register as a "new user" and verify your email address.

If you have any issues, please email support@testprepbooks.com

Dear Parent or Teacher,

Thank you again for purchasing this study guide for your child or student. We hope that we exceeded your expectations.

Our goal in creating this study guide was to introduce the student to the types of questions that will be found on their test. We also strove to make our practice questions as similar as possible to what the student will encounter on test day. With that being said, if you found something that you feel was not up to your standards, please send us an email and let us know.

We have study guides in a wide variety of fields. If you're interested in one for yourself or another one for your child, try searching for it on Amazon or send us an email.

Thanks Again and Happy Testing!
Product Development Team
info@studyguideteam.com

Made in United States
North Haven, CT
29 September 2023

42171104R00096